Monographs

of the Yale Center of Alcohol Studies

No. 2

Monographs of the
Yale Center of Alcohol Studies

Under the editorship of Mark Keller

The Yale Center of Alcohol Studies is a section of the Yale University Laboratory of Applied Biodynamics. The Monographs in this series report the results of original research in any of the scientific disciplines, whether carried out at Yale or elsewhere.

No. 1. Alcohol and the Jews. A Cultural Study of Drinking and Sobriety. By CHARLES R. SNYDER. $5.00

No. 2. Revolving Door. A Study of the Chronic Police Case Inebriate. By DAVID J. PITTMAN and C. WAYNE GORDON. $4.00

No. 3. Alcohol in Italian Culture. Food and Wine in Relation to Sobriety among Italians and Italian Americans. By GIORGIO LOLLI, EMIDIO SERIANNI, GRACE M. GOLDER and PIERPAOLO LUZZATTO-FEGIZ. $4.00

Revolving Door

BIBLIOGRAPHIC NOTE

The factual materials presented in this monograph parallel data used by David J. Pittman for his doctoral dissertation "The Chronic Police Case Inebriate" (University of Chicago, 1956). This monograph is not, however, a publication of that dissertation but a new work.

The materials contained in the section of Chapter 2 called "Criminal History" and in the Summary of the same chapter were published with little modification as the article "Criminal Careers of the Chronic Police Case Inebriate" in the QUARTERLY JOURNAL OF STUDIES ON ALCOHOL, Vol. 19, No. 2, June 1958.

Revolving Door

A Study of the Chronic Police Case Inebriate

BY

DAVID J. PITTMAN, PH.D.

AND

C. WAYNE GORDON, PH.D.

THE FREE PRESS

GLENCOE, ILLINOIS

PUBLICATIONS DIVISION:

YALE CENTER OF ALCOHOL STUDIES

NEW HAVEN, CONNECTICUT

Library of Congress catalog card number: 58–9166

MANUFACTURED IN THE UNITED STATES OF AMERICA BY
UNITED PRINTING SERVICES, INC.
NEW HAVEN, CONN.

TO OUR PARENTS

ISABELLE AND CALVIN

JAY AND LAURA

Study of the Chronic Police Case Inebriate

The Research Team

C. Wayne Gordon, Ph.D., Director
David J. Pittman, Ph.D., Associate Director
Thomas B. Richards, M.A., Interviewer
John Norris, M.D., Medical Consultant
Ralph Collins, M.D., Psychiatric Consultant
Lee Miller, M.D., Examining Physician

The Sponsors

The State Mental Health Commission of New York

and

The Health Association of Rochester and Monroe County

Contents

List of Tables

Acknowledgments

This research was carried out under the sponsorship of the Health Association of Rochester and Monroe County. It was made possible by a grant from the Mental Health Commission of the Department of Mental Hygiene, State of New York.

The authors wish to express their deep appreciation to Miss Marie Goulett, Executive Director of the Health Association of Rochester and Monroe County, and her staff for help in organizing and carrying out the research which began with the conception of the study and continued through the writing of the report. The authors are equally indebted to Mr. Raymond G. McCarthy, Director of Alcoholism Research for the New York State Mental Health Commission, for his help and support in all phases of the research.

The field work was performed by the Reverend Thomas Richards, Director of the Men's Service Center of Rochester. We are indebted in countless ways to Mr. Richards, but especially for his skillful interviewing of the subjects in the Monroe County Penitentiary. His wide experience and background knowledge of the men, combined with his patience and persistence in collecting the data, made his an outstanding contribution. We wish to thank the Board of Directors of the Men's Service Center for releasing him to participate in the study.

To Dr. John Norris, Chairman of the Alcoholism Committee of the Health Association of Rochester and Monroe County, we are indebted for continuous support and wise counsel. He served as Chairman of the Medical Subcommittee which planned the medical section of the study; he secured the services of Kodak Park Medical Division for laboratory analysis, attended the research conferences, and contributed in many other ways to the fulfillment of the project.

Dr. Lee Miller performed the medical examinations and made the analysis of the medical data. His sensitive and sympathetic handling of the physical examinations provided one of the major sources of social as well as medical information. Dr. William Sutton also performed some of the physical examinations after Dr. Miller had to leave the project for military service.

Dr. Ellis Soble and Dr. Harold Bonner, the latter Medical Director of the Rochester Alcoholism Clinic, also gave invaluable help; they served on the Medical Subcommittee, which planned the medical section of the interview schedule, and participated in all staff conferences. We wish also to thank Dr. Joe Howland, Chief of the Medical Division of the Atomic Energy Commission, who cooperated with Doctor Bonner on some experimental testing of the subjects with radioactive iodine.

Dr. Ralph Collins, consulting psychiatrist for the study, formulated sections of the interview schedule on family background and gave valuable aid in interpreting case material from the interviews.

To Mr. John McKenzie, Warden of the Monroe County Penitentiary; Mr. Sam Houston, Deputy Warden; Mr. William Veness, Identification Officer; and Dr. Felix Ratoli, physician, we owe much. Without the fine cooperation of Mr. McKenzie and his staff, the study could not have been made.

All of the personnel of the Health Association have contributed in some way. We are especially indebted to Miss Marian Wettrick, Health Education Secretary for the Committee on Alcoholism, who helped with the initial phase of the study; Mr. Louis Frasca, Health Education Secretary for the Committee on Alcoholism, who coordinated the data collection and suffered many of the headaches of smoothing out the data collecting in the early stages of the research; and Mr. Denez Gulyas, Program Director of the Committee on Alcoholism, who was responsible for coordinating the final phase of the study during the analysis and report writing. We appreciate the excellent work of Miss Eleanore Fisher in editing and typing the manuscript.

Professor Earl Loman Koos, former Chairman of the Department of Sociology, Rochester University, was in large part responsible for initiating the study. We are indebted to him for many suggestions and helpful criticisms in the early phase of the study.

Dean Morey Wantman of the University of Rochester, Dr. Lee Crump of the Atomic Energy Commission, and Dr. Mildred Kantor, County Health Department of St. Louis, Mo., all gave valuable statistical assistance.

Mrs. Anne Ludlow of the Sociology Department of the University of Rochester has given that combination of secretarial, editorial and moral assistance without which no research would ever prosper. Her contribution is immeasurable.

We wish to acknowledge the service of a member of Alcoholics Anonymous for transporting the laboratory samples from the penitentiary to Kodak Park Medical Division and of the Eastman Kodak Company for performing the laboratory analysis without charge.

We are grateful to the editorial staff of the Publications Division of the Yale Center of Alcohol Studies for aid in preparing this work for publication. Our thanks also to Marilyn Smith, graduate student in sociology, for helping prepare the case material included in the presentation.

Some division of labor may be noted. The formulation of the study design and the writing of Chapters 1 and 8 were carried out jointly. David Pittman performed the statistical analysis of the data and carried the major burden of writing the report; he wrote Chapters 2, 3, 4, 5 and 6. The general direction of the study, the supervision of data collection, the qualitative analysis of case histories, and the writing of Chapter 7 were done by Wayne Gordon.

The total manuscript or selected parts were read by a number of our peers in the academic profession. Professors Allison Davis, Norman Martin, Robert Hess, William Henry, and Bernice Neugarten of the University of Chicago's Committee on Human Development read and commented on parts of this material which appeared as the senior author's dissertation. Their interest and critical comments have added to the total formulation of the contents.

The ideas and theories represent the intermingled creations of the research team. Final responsibility for the contents of the report is shared by both writers.

C. WAYNE GORDON
DAVID J. PITTMAN

Departments of Education and Sociology,
University of California, Los Angeles

Departments of Sociology and Psychiatry,
Washington University and School of Medicine

September 1958

Foreword

This study has tried to answer several applied questions:

How many chronic alcoholics are we caring for in the Monroe County Penitentiary?

How large a part of the penitentiary population do they contitute?

How effective is this method of treatment? We know from other studies that many had returned to the penitentiary over and over again; but how many in Monroe County?

What physical and mental resources have they? Would they be employable if their alcoholism were controlled?

What use have they made of the other treatment resources of the community?

It was hoped that with these answers we would be able to plan the next steps which we should take as a community to better meet the needs of this part of our problem of alcoholism.

We believe the study to have been well planned as a team approach involving the disciplines of medicine, psychiatry and sociology. There have been many factors favoring reliable results. Two, especially memorable, are a considerate, humane, cooperative attitude on the part of the penitentiary staff; and previous constructive contact between the Reverend Thomas Richards who did the interviewing and the men interviewed.

We are grateful to the Mental Health Commission of the State of New York for the support which made this study possible, and for the invaluable advice of Mr. Raymond G. McCarthy in its planning and execution. We appreciate the cooperation of the Department of Sociology of the University of Rochester and the services of Doctor Pittman and Doctor Gordon; and the help of the Board of Directors of the Men's Service Center of Rochester in releasing for half his time their Director, the Reverend Thomas Richards, to do the interviewing.

JOHN NORRIS, M.D., *Chairman*
Committee on Alcoholism,
Health Association of Rochester
and Monroe County

Preface

The publication of the present monograph represents a significant stride toward the understanding of a very complex problem in human behavior and social organization. Previous writers have offered some important theoretical interpretations and have provided suggestive descriptive data on the men who constitute this problem. Doctors Pittman and Gordon have provided a valuable synthesis of previous work in this field as a point of departure for their own investigation. They have penetrated the wall of "pat response" which has so often surrounded the life histories of homeless men. The careful planning and skillful execution of their study greatly enhances the respect which their findings and interpretations command.

The significance of this study is not limited to its intrinsic findings. It represents a unique and exemplary community achievement. This work could not have been produced without smooth cooperation among a university, a community voluntary health association, a state tax-supported mental health agency, a county tax-supported department of corrections, a voluntary religious social service agency, and many individuals with diverse training and orientation. It is encouraging indeed to realize how effectively individual interests were integrated in this interdisciplinary and interorganizational effort.

The authors are behavioral scientists. They are seeking generalizations to explain processes of human behavior. They hope that the insights which they gain can be applied to the alleviation of human maladaptation. But as scientists, their primary concern is not with what behavior should be or should not be. They are concerned with basic facts and basic phenomena; what they are, how they know this, and what this means to them in the light of other information at their command. As scientists, their approach to problems in human behavior is an objective one, unclouded with emotional overtones.

For many persons, the subject of chronic inebriation, especially as represented in the men who populate our local jails, is associated with deepset emotional subjectivity and prejudice, supported by stereotyped misconception. Individuals and agencies responsible for dealing with this segment of the population have rarely been immune to the same feelings of moral condemnation which society at large has directed toward the homeless inebriate. Doctors Pittman and Gordon suggest that the behavior patterns which are manifested by these men are associated with certain characteristic experiences in the life history. These are complex experiences. They do not permit cause-and-effect explanations. But they do relate the dilemma of the chronic police case inebriate to the same type of group relationships which every human being experiences: the family, the church, the school, the community, and the job. They enable the reader to identify with these men and to see in them fellow human creatures whose experiences of socialization may vary only in degree from their own. The authors relate the present status of these men to social process and deprivation rather than personal failing or inadequacy. Thus they help to break down emotionally based prejudice and rejection at the same time that they bring us further on the continuum of greater objectivity and understanding.

ROBERT STRAUS, PH.D.
Professor of Medical Sociology,
University of Kentucky Medical Center,
Lexington, Kentucky

Chapter 1

PROBLEM AND METHOD

STATEMENT OF THE PROBLEM

PENAL INSTITUTIONS to which short-term commitments are made by minor courts find themselves taking custody of prisoners who have been convicted repeatedly for public intoxication. The treatment of these individuals by the penal institutions is at best casual and custodial. The repetitious jailing and release of these men as society's only response to the vexing problem they present has been aptly termed the revolving door policy. Rarely has any attempt been made to assess the potentialities of the inebriates for rehabilitation or treatment. In fact, an analogy can be made between contemporary society's philosophy and methods in dealing with chronic inebriates and the conditions and beliefs that Dorothea Dix discerned in the nineteenth century with respect to the mentally ill.

The present research is an analysis of the case studies of a random sample of all men who were sentenced at least twice to a penal institution on charges relating to public intoxication and who were incarcerated in the Monroe County Penitentiary during the year 1953–1954 when the investigation was conducted. The focus was on four major questions: (A) Who are the chronic police case inebriates in terms of major social characteristics? (B) What have been their socialization experiences? (C) What experiences have these men had with existent treatment and rehabilitation agencies in the community? (D) What bearing does repeated incarceration have on the problem of rehabilitating these men and reintegrating them within the community? It is hoped that this research will lay a foundation from which social action in this general problem area can proceed.

With the exception of traffic and parking violations, more people are charged in the United States with the violation of laws relating to public intoxication than with any other offense category. The Federal Bureau of Investigation's *Uniform Crime Reports,* which unfortunately do not cover arrests from all the manifold political jurisdictions in the country, report over a million arrests annually on

1

the charge of public intoxication or drunkenness. In New York State in the year 1954 court arraignments for public intoxication totaled 15,000 in New York City, 10,000 in Buffalo, 5,426 in Rochester, 2,200 in Syracuse, and 1,352 in Binghamton. In 1955, arrests for public intoxication or "disorderly conduct" totaled over 100,000 in Los Angeles, over 50,000 in Chicago, and around 40,000 in the District of Columbia. From these statistics Judge Murtagh concluded that "there are probably a half million Skid Row alcoholics throughout the country" (37).

Not only is public intoxication the most frequent offense category, but it provides the county or short-term penal institution with a significant number of incarcerated offenders. In the Monroe County, New York, Penitentiary, which receives offenders from 13 western New York counties, of the 1,919 inmates received in 1954, 70 per cent were charged with public intoxication. The same situation holds for the Onondaga County, New York, Penitentiary which receives offenders from 24 central New York counties: in 1954, of the 1,958 inmates received, 58 per cent were sentenced for public intoxication. The Westchester County Penitentiary reported that 44 per cent of its total of 1,559 commitments in 1954 were for public intoxication. The above statistics do not include the numerous offenses which may quite frequently be intimately associated with the excessive intake of alcohol, such as disorderly conduct, vagrancy, aggravated assault, and so forth. If these were included, then the above percentages would be increased considerably.

The chronic inebriate offender is only part of the larger grouping of over 4½ million men and women who have difficulties with the use of acohol, of whom more than a million are "alcoholics with complications" (28). Regardless of the exactitude of these statistics, the alcoholic population is obviously larger than those in mental hospitals, prisons and reformatories, homes for the aged and infirm, or persons with acute tuberculosis. This problem of excessive drinkers is the most serious current social problem in terms of its magnitude (41, *pp. 251–4*). Alcoholism and excessive drinking have never been rigidly dichotomized to the satisfaction of most students in the field of alcoholism research. This difficulty has been aptly phrased by Bacon.[1] "All alcoholics are problem drinkers, but not all problem drinkers are alcoholics." Some of the chronic inebriate

---

[1] Selden D. Bacon, public lecture on alcoholism, Le Moyne Conference on Alcoholism, Syracuse, New York, June 1955.

offenders are confirmed alcoholics; others are miscreants whose present use of alcohol is preliminary to confirmed alcoholism; and others are nonaddicted excessive drinkers who will never become alcoholics.

This research, then, is concerned with a group of excessive drinkers who may or may not be alcoholics, but whose drinking has involved them in difficulty with constituted sources of authority—the police, the courts, and the penal institutions. They are chronic offenders in the sense that the criterion for their selection for study has been at least two sentences to the short-term correctional institution. Their recidivism ranges from 2 to 100 incarcerations for each individual. In the Monroe County Penitentiary the inebriate recidivists are by far the majority. Of those sentenced for public intoxication in 1952, 82 per cent were serving their second or further penalty in the institution. They represent a hard core of individuals who are involved in a circular process of arrest, incarceration, release and rearrest for public intoxication, and a group for whom the penal sanctions of the society have failed along with the existent community resources for rehabilitation.

The basic conclusion to be derived is that the knowledge concerning this category—chronic police case inebriate—is incomplete. In the research on inebriety, there is no complete sociological description of the chronic police case inebriates as a category or of their developmental profiles, although partial descriptive and developmental accounts can be found. For example, Floch (18) in his study of 276 abnormal drinkers sentenced to the Detroit House of Corrections between 1933 and 1944 is more concerned with the application of the Bowman–Jellinek classification schedule to the inebriates than in a complete social-psychological description of the inmates. His problem is one of categorizing the inebriate as a stupid, discordant or compensatory drinker and then comparing the three groups. These three classifications, especially "stupid," leave much to be desired by the student of drinking behavior. The Utah State Board on Alcoholism (61) in cooperation with the University of Utah School of Social Work undertook a study designed to determine the effects, deterrent or rehabilitative, of arrests, fines and incarceration on a group of repeatedly jailed inebriates in Salt Lake City. Court and prison records of the offenders were analyzed to determine whether the inebriates were a resident problem, whether the problem was one of continuing duration, and what its financial aspects were. Only limited insight is given concerning the social characteristics of the offenders and the developmental profile of the deviant behavior. Bacon's (3) study, based on a survey of all persons arrested for public intoxication in a 5-week period in five large and three small towns in Connecticut in 1942 and supplemented by an analysis of all other arrests on any charge in the same period in the same area, is an excellent example of the sociological approach to the problem. His group of inebriates contains more than the police court habitués who are our concern but the latter group is included. The characteristic arrested inebriate is typically a middle-aged man marked by undersocialization. He belongs to and participates in only a minimum of social groupings and activities. Bacon's thesis is that "marked 'undersocialization' preceded the onset of inebriety, that inebriety was a symptom of this condition and an aggravation strengthening its continuance." However, the study leaves unanswered many questions relating not only to the general grouping of inebriates but to the particular category of chronic police case inebriates. The social characterization is incomplete, and the author does not concern himself with characteristic developmental profiles.

More closely related to the present study is Smith's (44) analysis of the individuals arraigned three or more times for public intoxication in the Syracuse Court of Special Sessions with special emphasis on the cost to the community as viewed through the records of the Social Service Exchange.

Insights concerning the public inebriate can be gleaned from studies of related groups such as the homeless man and patients seen in private and public alcoholism clinics. Also, critical studies of various approaches to research on alcoholism can be valuable in determining a frame of reference for further study.

The "homeless" man group to a large extent overlaps that of the chronic police case inebriate. Although no accurate statistics are available from investigations of homeless men on how many are police court habitués for intoxication, there is every reason to believe that a large proportion of them follow the "Skid Row to jail to Skid Row to jail" pattern. However, the studies of Sutherland and Locke (53), Anderson (2), Straus (46), and Straus and McCarthy (50) all indicate that the two groups are not identical. Nevertheless, these studies have implications for the present investigation—particularly that of Straus (46) who attempted, through interviews with 203 homeless men at a Salvation Army shelter in New Haven, to isolate significant characteristics of the homeless man and to discern whether these were also characteristic of the excessive drinker. He found, outstandingly, that the homeless man is undersocialized (which was also Bacon's conclusion concerning the inebriate). This can be discerned in the homeless man's lack of participation in socially created and organized activities which would bring him into contact with other individuals. However, Straus does not spell out the developmental history of the homeless man's socialization process except in a general way for the family. The crucial role of the peer group in socialization is not discussed. Of more interest is the insight of Straus on the role of the peer group for the homeless man in his present situation. He states that "for them one of the chief functions of drinking was to provide an easy introduction to congenial companions," and that drinking is "with the boys." A more exact description of drinking groups has been given by Jackson and Connor (25), who classified the "Skid Road" society as made up of permanent resident nondrinking groups, older alcoholic groups, the "winos," and the "lushes" (the latter being the prestige group). But they did not attempt to analyze the functional roles these cliques play in the life history of the homeless man.

The study with most relevance for the present research is that of Straus and McCarthy (50), which presents evidence to counteract the stereotype that pictures the inebriate in our culture either as a derelict who should be confined to jail or to a Skid Row existence, or as an individual with a serious mental aberration requiring hospitalization. There is a lack of evidence to show that the homeless man who is characterized by excessive drinking exhibits the criteria of alcohol addiction. Straus and McCarthy's survey of the drinking patterns of 444 homeless men who used shelter facilities on the New York Bowery reveals an impressive number whose life is dominated by pathological drinking but who are not addicted to alcohol. They do not seek the maximum effect of alcohol but are rather "plateau drinkers" whose use of alcohol is an established pattern of their life activities.

In this review of the literature relevant for the present investigation, two other studies have significance. The police case inebriate is different in his external social characteristics from the patients seen in outpatient alcoholism clinics, who are prone to show greater signs of social stability and integration. This is confirmed in a study

of clinic patients by Straus and Bacon (49). For students of personality the critical reviews by Sutherland, Schroeder and Tordella
(54) and by Syme (55) will be especially interesting. After review-
ing all studies in which a variety of techniques such as the Rorschach
or the Thematic Apperception were used, these investigators came
to the conclusion that it has not been possible to differentiate an
alcoholic personality prior to or after alcoholism develops. The im-
plication is that alcoholics are not a homogeneous group but are
composed of subgroupings which should be differentiated for further study.

Our review indicates that there is no complete descriptive account
of the chronic police case inebriate as a group, though partial pictures have been given of this and related groups such as the "homeless man." There is no information concerning the developmental
profiles of this category. However, crucial leads for research into
this group are provided in other studies—especially the utilization
of the concepts of socialization and peer group.

From this survey of the literature concerned with the police case
inebriate and related groups, it is possible to outline the areas in
which our knowledge is inadequate as follows:

1. There is no complete sociological description of the institutional population who are the chronic police case inebriates.

2. There is limited information concerning the developmental
history of the inebriates.

A. Knowledge concerning the early socialization experiences in
the family of orientation is the most complete concerning inebriates
who have been patients in clinics and hospitals.

B. The influences of the peer groups from childhood, but in particular from adolescence, to later maturity have been only superfi-
cially analyzed.

3. There are no systematic studies of a significant number of
life histories of inebriates; as a consequence, few developmental
profiles are available. This is particularly true in reference to drinking histories as related to crucial life experiences.

4. On a more practical plane, there is no systematic body of
knowledge concerning this category which penal officials, social
workers, judges and others can consult. Practical workers in the
field have little information from which rehabilitative action can
proceed. As a result, the discharged individual may or may not find
his way to a clinic or other services which will help him to make a

more satisfactory adjustment to the community and his problem. The fact that many individuals are repeatedly committed to such penal institutions would indicate that they have not found the way to agencies which offer therapy.

It is hoped that the present research, a sociological study of the life experiences of these men, will contribute to both the theoretical and substantive knowledge in this field.

The Theoretical Background

The present research uses as its foundation the social-problem approach which has been widely employed in sociology to investigate problem or deviant-behavior groups such as drug addicts, juvenile delinquents, homeless men, and alcoholics. In this approach a selection of categories is made by which a problem group can be described in terms of age, sex, nationality, race, urban–rural background, marital status, educational attainment, occupation, income, religion, and other relevant categories. A comparison can be made between the distribution of these traits in the problem groups and other selected groups, e.g., the general population or comparable and noncomparable problem groups. Utilizing this technique, studies have been made of alcoholics in state hospitals, police case drunkards, patients of private physicians, patients at alcoholism clinics, and members of various Alcoholics Anonymous groups.

The social-problem approach, however, is not expansive enough in area for the study of problem groups. The recent trend is to employ the broader social–psychological approach. For example, research concerning alcoholic groups has moved from the purely descriptive to a more analytical level. The expanded approach is evidenced in the gathering of data in such areas as drinking patterns, behavior in stress situations, primary and secondary group roles, and occupational and marital attitudes. In viewing a social problem, the concern is now more with the operation of social organization and cultural phenomena on individual and group behavior and the crucial role of social relationships both for behavioral development and change in individuals.[2]

From a survey of some of the numerous studies which have focused on deviant behavior, ranging from sexual pathologies to

[2] This discussion of the social-problem approach relies heavily on the lucid statement (4) of Selden D. Bacon, Director, Yale Center of Alcohol Studies.

criminal behavior, it is believed that a most profitable area of research for the developmental aspects of inebriety and deviant behavior in general is found in the complex of the socialization process.

The theoretical formulation of this research study will be cast in terms of the continuous socialization process by which all members of a society are affected. This formulation is eclectic in nature, originating in the writings of Charles Horton Cooley (11), Allison Davis (14, *pp. 137–70, 208–27*), John Dollard (35), and Robert J. Havighurst (23). The contribution of Cooley is that of the primary group, and that of Havighurst, the concept of developmental tasks. The writings of Davis and Dollard concerning the socialization of the child in American society and the crucial role of the peer group in personality development provided a basis for the advancement of the hypotheses of this study.

All adult functioning members of society have undergone a socialization process in which they become transformed from the vegetating organisms they are at birth to persons who participate in the groups of the culture. In this continuing process the individual learns:

1. The rules of society including those of the subcultural groups of which he is a member;

2. The ways in which goals may be achieved;

3. The socially approved means of securing personality-need gratifications;

4. The socially approved means of alleviating anxiety, tension and frustration;

5. The social roles prevailing in the society and in the subcultural groups of which he is a member.

Socialization of all organisms is dependent upon the constantly operating variable, the primary groups. Empirically these become the family of orientation, the child play group, and the adolescent peer group; we can measure the presence or absence of these groups, but in a qualitative sense the effects of these groups on individual personality development is more difficult to grasp.

The primary groups, however, perform certain well-defined functions for the individual in his developmental history. These may be categorized as the development of two types of task roles:

1. There are those tasks for continued primary-group associations which serve in the maintenance of personality needs such as securi-

ty, response, recognition and emotional support. In personality formation the individual's primary groups are essential in the formation of ego ideals and in providing identification models. Furthermore, the individual's sense of identity is nurtured and developed in the primary groups. For individuals to function in our society, socialized anxiety must be instilled, but effective channels must, also, be constructed in the continuing primary groups for the reduction of anxiety in periods of crisis. Thus, the primary groups in which the individual exists serve self-needs positively and alleviate his distress.

2. There are secondary group roles which call for achievement under demanding situations. Experiences in primary task roles are sometimes referred to as developmental skills. Specific secondary role demands for which primary group association is a precondition are (A) work or occupational roles; (B) marital roles; (C) educational roles. Actually the personality must integrate both the primary and secondary group roles for complete socialization to occur.

The central focus of the present investigation will be concerned with the chronic police case inebriates' initial experience of primary group associations, and their continued existence as determinants of performance in secondary group roles.

Hypotheses

For the study of the chronic police case inebriate group the following hypotheses are proposed:

I. The chronic police case inebriate is a category with definable sociocultural attributes such as age, nationality, race, urban–rural background, marital status, educational attainment, occupation, religion, previous criminal record, social class membership, and mobility.

A. These inebriates are members of the lower socioeconomic group which has the greatest vulnerability to arrest.

B. The group is geographically mobile.

C. Its members possess a low order of occupational skills.

D. Their educational attainment is limited to grammar school or incomplete high-school training.

E. They do not constitute a culturally homogeneous category.

F. For the lower-class white and Negro in the sample, geographic mobility from rural areas to urban centers will be the most crucial cultural factor. Their cultural marginality in the city is reflected in their high vulnerability to arrest for public intoxication.[3]

II. The chronic police case inebriate's developmental history is marked by qualitative and quantitative undersocialization.[4]

A. This inebriate has been undersocialized in his family of orientation.

Data to test hypothesis *II-A:* The most important socializing agent is the family. In the primary group of the family the crucial element for the socialization of the child is not the material aspects of the grouping but the quality of the relationship and, more important, how the individual subjectively experiences and expresses it. In the present study, the following information was obtained to test the hypothesis:

1. Structural features of the family of orientation: broken and unbroken; death of parents; and sibling position.

2. Geographical and vertical mobility of the family.

3. Index of Family Integration (adaptation–integration).[5]

4. Goals–aspirations of the family for the child.

5. Individual attitude toward family of orientation. (Here depth questions were used to identify the quality of the relationship in the family.)

6. Individual's participation in the family of orientation.

B. The chronic police case inebriate lacked participation in and the socializing influence of the adolescent peer group.

Data to test hypothesis *II-B:*

1. Amount and quality of peer group participation and satisfaction.

2. Heterosexual relationships as related to peer groups.

3. Drinking experience as related to peer groups.

---

[3] The present study deals only with men seen in a Northern urban center. There is no reason to believe that those who migrate to other areas are in any way different; thus the findings will be applicable generally.

[4] By undersocialization we mean that the person's life history is characterized by limited participation in the primary groups which are necessary for personality formation, by minimum participation in social activities, and by inadequate opportunities for sharing experiences with others. His life history is one that has been and continues to be deficient in membership in those associations of sharing that are found in the family of orientation and procreation, in the peer groups that stretch from preadolescence to old age, and in community activities.

[5] This study has made use of certain items of the scale of Family Integration and Adaptation developed by Ruth Shoule Cavan; it is reproduced completely in Burgess and Locke (9, *pp.* 781–4).

4. Goals as related to peer groups.

C. In adulthood, due to undersocialization, the chronic police case inebriate lacks experience in primary task roles which would promote his adaptation in secondary task roles (work, marital and educational roles).

Data to test hypothesis *II-C*:

1. Work roles: the father's occupational role, work adaptation, and attitudes toward work; subject's first work experience and succeeding experience; stability of subject's employment.

2. Marital roles: dating, courtship complex, marriage, sexual experiences, parental models, husband–wife models, peer group interaction with opposite sex.

3. Educational roles: special reference to school achievement and reasons for leaving school; family attitude toward school.

4. Geographic mobility data.

III. Chronic inebriety is developmental in nature and involves a process of drifting from abstinence or social or controlled drinking to excessive drinking, reaching the culmination of uncontrolled drinking. A concomitant development in the chronic police case inebriate is the institutionalization of the individual in dependency. Involved in both institutionalization and the drinking drift are the occurrence of crisis situations, resulting from inability to perform primary and secondary group roles, which leads to further inability to enact these roles. Furthermore there are two career patterns in public intoxication, differentiated by age, which may be referred to as the Early Skid and the Late Skid career patterns.

Data to test hypothesis *III*:

1. Drinking histories in relation to age of onset of drinking.

2. Arrest and incarceration records.

3. Histories of contact with institutional facilities (military service, Merchant Marine, Civilian Conservation Corps, hospitals, and so forth).

IV. For the chronic police case inebriates, as a subgroup in a lower-class social system characterized by undersocialization, inebriety functions as a mechanism for securing personality need gratifications unobtainable in socially sanctioned channels and for reducing anxiety generated by the inability to perform secondary roles. The structural context in which this occurs is the drinking group of the chronic police case inebriate. In contrast to certain other categories of alcoholics (e.g., many members of Alcoholics

Anonymous) who were primarily solitary drinkers, these men are
group drinkers.

Data to test hypothesis *IV*:

1. First use of alcohol related to the context of the situation.

2. Individual's attitude toward the use of alcohol.

3. Drinking companions. Are drinking companions viewed as
a group?

THE SAMPLE

This is a study of the chronic police case inebriate conducted at
the Monroe County Penitentiary, Rochester, during a period of 1
year from October 1953 through September 1954. The sampling
universe consisted of all commitments in this period.[6] This universe
totaled 828 cases. Beginning with a random number, every fourth
case was sampled which met the following criteria:

1. Male. Females were eliminated because of the small number
committed for public intoxication at this institution. The average
is generally around 20 per year.

2. Sentenced to the Monroe County Penitentiary for public intoxication from Monroe County or the City of Rochester. This was
necessary because 13 other western New York counties used this
penitentiary for some but not all of their convictions for public
intoxication. Thus a selective bias may be in operation in reference
to non-Monroe County offenders.

3. Recidivist—having served at least one previous sentence at
some short-term correctional institution on a charge of public intoxication. Examination of incarceration records reveals that these
jailings are not widely separated in time. This criterion eliminates
the first-conviction category from consideration (about 18 per cent
of the total Monroe County commitments in 1951 and 1952).

4. Sentenced for a period of 30 days or more. A frequency distribution of length of sentence of the 1952 public intoxication group
was constructed after an examination of records revealed variations
in the length of sentence depending upon two variables—City of
Rochester or Monroe County conviction, and the sentencing judge.
For sampling purposes all public intoxication offenders serving 29
days or less were excluded. It was believed that this group would

---

[6] An examination of commitment records of the preceding 4 years (1948–1951)
revealed that there had been a variation of less than 100 in total commitments and
less than 50 in public intoxication cases per year.

have insufficient time for recovery from acute effects of the last bout, physical examination, laboratory tests, and the social history inquiry.

A total of 187 cases was thus obtained for the sample.

METHOD

A detailed case history was obtained from each of the 187 men in the sample. The information was recorded on an interview schedule composed of eight sections: (1) Family Background and Relationships; (2) Family Dynamics; (3) Educational Background; (4) Occupational Data; (5) Mobility Pattern; (6) Institutional Living; (7) Marital Status; and (8) Drinking Pattern. Each case has a 1-page summary by the interviewer plus a drinking history chart. The interview, conducted in one session, lasted from 2 to 4 hours.

The interviews were scheduled and completed after the prisoners had had a uniform period for "drying out" and adjustment to penitentiary life. Since this was a captive group, there was no problem regarding the choice of the sample or their availability for study. The interview, which was conducted during the working hours of the inmates, induced a desire on the part of many who were not selected by the sampling procedure to cooperate, since it would have provided a break in the monotonous routine of penal life or release from duties at the pig farm or from other onerous tasks. Only 27 men refused to be interviewed and substitutes had to be chosen. Many inmates volunteered for interview when not selected, in the belief that the interviewer would be able to help them with their problems or in their adjustment to the community upon their release.

A complete medical examination, including laboratory tests, was planned for each man in the sample. A total of 148 medical examinations was obtained; thus 21 per cent of the sample did not receive medical examinations. Of these, approximately one-third were due to refusal and the others could not be carried out because of the departure of the examining physician before completion of the project.

Analysis of Data

The basic technique in the analysis of the data is a frequency count of the schedule item responses. In the original construction of the interview schedule, an attempt was made to design questions which were amenable to answer by a limited number of responses. For this reason, open-ended and depth interview questions were kept at a minimum. The basic category used in the analysis is that of the chronological age of the inmates. Also used when deemed applicable are race, nationality background, religious affiliation, educational attainment, occupational classification, adolescent adjustment, marital status, social class origin, and the criminal record of the individual.

The first analysis of the raw data yielded a frequency distribution of all the 162 items in the schedule by 4 major age divisions: less than 35 years; 35–44; 45–54, and 55 or older. Items were further analyzed according to the other basic categories previously mentioned.

Although this study has no formal control group in the experimental sense, control groups for comparison are available from other studies, and comparisons may be drawn between subgroupings in the sample.

The controls can be listed as follows: (1) The general population, data on which can be obtained from the United States Bureau of the Census. (2) Empirical studies of groups who evidence a drinking problem. Particularly valuable here are the studies of the social characteristics of individuals who attend alcoholism clinics, since it is assumed with reason that clinic patients represent different classes from those included in the chronic police case inebriate category. This category of studies of clinic patients includes the study by Straus and Bacon (49) on clinic patients covering a diverse geographic area. (3) When applicable, the results of general sociological studies can be used to compare the socialization experiences of these individuals with those of middle-class high-school students (21) or members of a lower-class teen-age gang (64).

Limitations of the Design

In retrospect, the researcher is always able to discern areas of his investigation which, given more favorable conditions such as time, financial support, and more precise tools for the analysis of behavior, could have been dealt with more completely. It is assumed that the above is an inherent limitation which is applicable to most studies in the field of human behavior. It must be noted, however, that the present investigation suffers from certain limitations of design as well.

The material obtained from the respondents represents the results of a "one shot" interview and has the limitations that are generally attached to a single interview. However, a decision was made at the beginning of this research that extensive coverage of a large sample would be emphasized over the intensive analysis of a few cases. A survey of the literature revealed that several cases of the most extreme type of chronic public inebriates had been reported but these did not seem to present a typical picture of the class.

Interview responses of the subjects in reference to their experience in the family of orientation are felt to be the most inadequate feature of the study. This is true for several reasons. First, the median age of the group is high—48, and the events that occurred several decades ago are subject to the selective factors of memory and distortions in perception that occur with the passage of time. It should be emphasized that these distortions are not due to an "alcoholic fog," since sufficient time was given for recovery to occur, or to deterioration, either physical or psychological, of the cognitive processes. If there is deterioration, it is of a social order, in that family experiences are part of a preexisting field of behavior that no longer has any meaning for them in their present external reality.

Early in the investigation it was discerned that the peer-group norms among the chronic police case inebriates restricted the amount and significance of material an individual is allowed to give an outsider concerning his present position. In fact, on Skid Row, where the majority of the individuals are located in social space, conversation does not focus around the previous activities and past experiences of the individual as it relates to his early socialization. The norms in general dictate that the inebriate take responsibility for his present situation and not blame the difficulty on the social and economic pressures of the environment or on his family of orientation.

Chapter 2

THE SOCIOCULTURAL PROFILE

THE OFFENSE CATEGORY

THE PURPOSE of this chapter is to present a profile of the relevant social and cultural attributes of the chronic police case inebriate. Thus, it is addressed to the basic question formulated earlier: Who are these men in terms of their significant characteristics?

The chronic police case inebriates are a category of individuals who have their common anchor in violations of the legal norms of society in reference to the use of alcohol. One of the unsettled arguments in the field of criminology concerns the utility of studying a criminal offense category, such as public intoxication, forgery or homicide. The negative point of view is built around the position that crime, as legally defined, is not a significant behavior category because persons convicted of violating specific criminal statutes do not form a representative sample of all those who violate that law. This fact has long been recognized by behavior scientists who are aware that only a portion of those who actually offend against the law are apprehended and convicted. Another objection to the study of criminal offense categories is that, since they are legal categories, they are not categories of behavior amenable to the scientific study of human behavior in general and of social control in particular.

This latter position has been counterattacked by the criminologist, Paul Tappan (57), who argues that the study of criminal offense categories by sociologists in general and criminologists in particular is feasible (a) because convicted criminals are the best representatives available of those who in actuality have violated the law and (b) because "The criminal law establishes substantive norms of behavior, standing more clear cut, specific and detailed than the norms in any other category of social control." Sociologists do not hesitate to deal with middle-class values and norms of cleanliness, achievement, sexual rigidity, and orderliness, yet these are hardly so clearly defined as the criminal statutes of our society. In fact, the transitional classes of upper-lower and lower-middle may show varying degrees of adherence to these norms, depending upon the direction of their mobility. Furthermore, criminal law expresses the general sentiments of the group in reference to how the individual should act in defined situations. As behavior occurs and is learned through interaction, criminal law is formulated in the interaction of groups and thus reflects the basic values of the society. When sociologists discuss American values they are referring primarily to those of middle-class society. The same holds for criminal law, which is not only the product of the mores but of the middle-class dominated legislative bodies. Thus, an offense category is the closest approximation that can be achieved to a specifically defined behavior category. If it becomes distorted, this is due to the impingement of uncontrollable factors such as policemen, attorneys, judges and other societal representatives who reclassify the individual after the commission of the act.

The chronic police case inebriate category consists of individuals with definable sociocultural traits such as age, nationality background, race, urban–rural background, marital status, religion, educational attainment, occupational skills, social class background, mobility, and previous criminal record. It is to these factors that we shall now direct our attention.

Age

Age is one of the crucial attributes that differentiate the chronic police case inebriates from all other offender groups. The age curve of individuals committed to short-term penal institutions for public intoxication is skewed toward the middle-age brackets, whereas commitments for such offenses as automobile theft, robbery, burglary and reckless driving involve chiefly individuals under age 25 (52, pp. 107–11).

This disproportionate distribution can be explained in terms of the developmental nature of the offense of public intoxication. A man generally does not become a problem drinker, enmeshed in difficulty with authority as represented by the police, overnight. A single episode of intoxication does not necessarily mobilize the police powers of the community as one act of car theft will. This is due, of course, to the fact that public intoxication is not viewed as seriously as theft of an automobile. This distinction is recognized in the legal code by the former being classified as a misdemeanor for which the individual will not lose his civil rights if convicted, while the latter is defined as a felony portending loss of civil rights.

TABLE 1.—*Age Distribution of the Sample Compared to the General Population and Alcoholism Clinic Patients*

Age (Years)	Sample		General Population[1]		Clinic Patients[2]	
	N	%	N	%	N	%
15–34	19	10	65,045	37	466	24
35–44	49	27	32,775	19	836	42
45–54	68	36	29,860	17	510	26
55 and over	51	27	46,990	27	171	8
Mean		47.7				41.2
Median		48.5				40.5
Totals	187	100	174,670	100	1,983	100

[1] Male inhabitants of Monroe County, New York, aged over 14 years, 1950. Source: 1950 United States Census of Population, "New York: Detailed Characteristics," Bulletin PB–32, Table 41, pp. 32–146.

[2] Source: Straus and Bacon (49, p. 242).

Thus, chronic inebriation is developmental in nature and reaches its culmination in middle age. This is not to say, however, that the warning signs of difficulty with alcohol do not occur earlier in the life history of the individual.

Table 1 presents a comparison of the age distribution of the present sample with males over 14 years of age in Monroe County and the alcoholism clinic patients in the Straus and Bacon study. Certain differences are immediately noticeable. The age of the incarcerated inebriates[1] is higher than that of the patients seen in the alcoholism clinics, and significantly higher than that of males over 14 in the general population. The average age of the inmates is 47.7 years and the median age is 48.5. The age range is from 19 to 78 with the heaviest concentration (54.5 per cent) in the ages between 40 and 55.

Table 2 summarizes age data from seven samples of uncontrolled drinkers. The lowest mean age and lowest percentage over 50 years of age was found in 1,983 alcoholism clinic patients who show strong signs of social stability when compared with other groups evidencing drinking problems (49). Bacon's (3) sample of 1,196 inebriates arrested in Connecticut in 1942 and the Salt Lake City sample (61) of 580 men arrested for drunkenness show mean ages that are almost identical, 43.1 and 43.4. In both studies about one-fourth of the men were over 50 years of age. The study (46) of 203 homeless men in a New Haven shelter revealed a mean age of 45.5 years,

[1] To avoid some repetition of "chronic police case inebriate," terms such as "incarcerated inebriate" or "the sample" will be substituted where convenient and not liable to ambiguity.

TABLE 2.—*Mean Ages and Per Cent Aged 50 Years and Older in Present Sample and in Six Samples[1] of Uncontrolled Drinkers*

	Mean Age (Years)	% Aged 50 and Older
187 Penitentiary inmates, present study	47.7	45
1,983 Alcoholism clinic patients	41.2	19
1,196 Arrested inebriates, Connecticut, 1942	43.1	25
580 Men arrested for drunkenness, Salt Lake City	43.4	28
309 First admissions for alcoholism without psychosis	44.9	29
203 Homeless men	45.5	28
784 First admissions with alcoholic psychoses, 1948	47.8	44

[1] Source: Straus and Bacon (49, p. 242).

and 28 per cent 50 years or older. Malzberg found that the average age of male first admissions for alcoholism without psychosis in New York was 44.9 years, and more than one-fourth are 50 years of age and older; while in a group admitted with alcoholic psychoses, the mean age was higher (47.8), and 44 per cent were 50 years of age or older.[2]

It should be noted that the chronic inebriate inmates of the Monroe County Penitentiary comprise one of the oldest groups to be studied, and they have the highest percentage of men aged 50 years or older. Their mean age is nearly that found by Malzberg in male first admissions for alcoholic psychoses, and higher than that of the two arrested groups. The difference between the two arrested groups and the present sample in percentage over 50 is statistically significant. The high median and mean ages and the large number of men who are at least 50 years old would appear to have extreme significance in any social action plan. However, the chronic police case inebriate is older as the result of the operation of definable social factors.

The older age of the chronic incarcerated inebriate can be explained in terms of the fact that jailing results from a complex of social and economic factors. Unless the individual is completely without personal and financial resources, jailing is the last method used to cope with the problem of constant inebriation. Upon first arrest for intoxication, the penalty may be no more than a reprimand or a fine; or an interested party, such as the local Alcoholics Anonymous group, an employer, or family member may intervene in the court process to ask for special treatment for the offender. Constant jailing occurs when the personal resources of the individual are at

[2] Cited from Straus and Bacon (49).

a minimum, when other agencies and individuals have despaired of helping in the situation, or when, in summary, the individual has literally "hit bottom." But the process of "hitting bottom" is developmental; it accelerates at middle age when the personal resources of the individual are reaching ebbtide.

Age selectivity also occurs in terms of police action in reference to the drunken person. The younger offender is frequently not arrested but may be assisted to his home by the policeman. Or, if he is brought to the police station "tank," he is frequently "sunrised" by the police, i.e., he is released in the morning without being formally booked. The charge is thus dismissed before it reaches the judge.

The peer group norms of the inebriates in their natural habitat on Skid Row place an extreme negative value on the entrance of younger individuals into the drinking cliques or "bottle gangs," as they are frequently called. Particularly, individuals under 30 who exhibit signs of becoming members of the Skid Row groups are not accepted by the older members. They are asked to leave the area, to find a more desirable way of existence, and if necessary are refused complete social interaction.

Racial Background

Studies in criminology of categoric risks for arrest and incarceration over many decades have shown that Negroes are more vulnerable than whites. Various explanations have been advanced for this fact, all centering around two basic factors. First, in American society, both North and South, the Negro is a victim of discriminatory practices and differential police action, which lead to his being arrested more frequently than comparable members of other groups in the society. Second, the Negro, because he is denied full access to rights and privileges in the educational and economic realm, is predominantly a member of those lower-class groupings in the society who are also more vulnerable to police action. This inequity is magnified by the existence of divergent cultural norms and values in the Negro lower-class society which conflict with the basic middle-class values and norms. In the lower-class group, the external release of aggression is an accepted mode of behavior in contrast to middle-class internalization of aggression. The cultural pattern of the lower-class Negro group does not place negative sanctions on the use of alcohol, and this, coupled with the pattern of aggres-

TABLE 3.—*Racial Classification, by Age Classes*

Age	Whites		Negroes		Total
(Years)	N	%	N	%	N
Under 35	10	53	9	47	19
35–44	35	73	13	27	48
45–54	58	85	10	15	68
55 and over	49	96	2	4	51
Totals[1]	152	82	34	18	186

[1] One Indian has been eliminated from this tabulation.

sion release, leads many into difficulty with the constituted sources of authority.

The Negro inebriate forms a substantial subgroup of the inmate population. Table 3 reveals that 82 per cent of the offenders are white and 18 per cent Negro, whereas in the population of Monroe County in 1950 fewer than 2 per cent were Negroes. Moreover, the Negro inebriates are much younger than the whites. In the youngest age class, under 35 years, the numbers in the two groups are approximately equal. In fact, around two-thirds of the Negroes are under 45 years of age, while only some 30 per cent of the whites are below 45. Thus, there is not only a disproportionate number of Negroes, but they are decidedly younger than their white counterparts.

The age differential and the high proportion of Negro offenders in the sample can be explained partly in terms of the migration trends in central and western New York State during the last 15 years. Negroes, as demographers have noted, have been migrating from the rural areas of the South, from which they have been displaced by the technological innovations of the past 4 decades, to the urban industrial centers in the Northeast and Midwest and, more recently, to the West Coast. However, only in the last decades have a signifi-cant number of Negroes found their way to central and western New York, with the possible exception of Buffalo. Due to the press-ing need for a labor supply for fruit and farming operations during the summer harvests, Negroes were originally recruited in the South to do the seasonal work abandoned by the Italians who had moved up the social class escalator and were no longer available. Many of the Negroes thus brought into the region did not return to the South at the end of the harvest season but instead drifted into the urban centers such as Rochester and Syracuse. Both of these cities recorded an increase of more than 100 per cent in their Negro population in the 1950 census over 1940. The process of accommodation in this area to the sizable increase in Negro population is just beginning.

The records show that of the 34 Negroes in the sample only 2 were born in New York State; the majority are from southern rural or small-town residences and of lower-class origin. Twenty-one of them were reared exclusively in rural or small-town places and had little prior experience with urban situations. In some cases their migration to northern areas was precipitated by difficulty with the legal system in the South, but the primary motivating force must be sought in their search for economic opportunity.

These Negroes represent basically a group which is attempting to bridge the gap between two quite alien cultures—the first, a rural or small-town paternalistic culture, the second, a complex urban technological culture. In the original milieu their excessive drinking may have been viewed as expected behavior and treated with a degree of paternalistic toleration by the employer or the police. In their new environment the definition attached to the same behavior both by themselves and the authorities is markedly different. For the person attempting to adjust to the new culture, the strains may be so great that his drinking increases to provide release from the frustrations encountered; or, separated from rigid primary-group ties of the *gemeinschaft* type of community in the South, the norms governing behavior are relaxed. At least, the generalization may be made that drinking in excessive amounts is one mode of adaptation to the new urban culture. The Negro offender in the new community also finds himself in a perilous position in relation to the authorities. Without friends and financial resources, and at times facing an unfriendly court desirous of doing something about these "no-good migrants," he is used as an example to others, to deter them from improper behavior, by being incarcerated in the county penitentiary.

From the above analysis, it is only logical to conclude that the Negro inebriate is one whose excessive use of alcohol is symptomatic of lack of adjustment to a new cultural environment, and also of the lack of any community interest in aiding him to achieve this adjustment. It seems safe to predict that, given the continued migration of young Negroes to this area, the differences in cultural environment, the difficulties of Negroes in being accepted into community life, and the attitudes toward and lack of comprehension of their cultural patterns by the authority structure, an increasing number of Negroes will be incarcerated as chronic inebriates in the short-term penal institution.

Nationality

Ethnic group affiliation is one of the major determinants of the cultural milieu in which the individual is socialized. It equips him with basic attitudes and values that form his personality structure. Ethnic group identification may be denied by an individual later in his life career, but its mark remains on the personality in many ways discernible to the behavior scientist.

Previous studies in the field of alcoholism have shown the crucial role which cultural background and attitudes play in alcohol addiction. Cultural attitudes define who may use alcohol, how and when they may use it, and above all, the mental set of the individual toward alcohol. Numerous investigators have noted that different cultural groups have extremely divergent rates of alcoholism.[3] For example, Irish groups are marked by high rates of alcohol addiction in this country; Italians have low rates. However, it is not in place here to explain the differences that exist among cultural groups, but rather to determine whether the general trends observed among them hold also in the incarcerated population.

Comparable statistics for an incarcerated population, from which it could be determined whether the nationality affiliations of the present sample are typical, do not exist. In fact, since the Bureau of the Census reports the nationality status only of the foreign born, and since there is an absence of reliable data on the nationality composition of the general population, the researcher's task is complicated when attempting to assess the significance of his data. However, general trends can be determined concerning those nationality groups which have the highest vulnerability to involvement in alcohol-related offenses.

Table 4 reveals that two nationality groups, the English and the Irish, are most heavily represented in the sample. The English group can be explained in terms of three major factors: First, given the settlement pattern of the area, the group is represented with a considerable degree of frequency in the general population. Second, an examination of the cultural patterns of this group shows a high

[3] For an extensive discussion of this topic see, e.g., Snyder (45).

TABLE 4.—*Nationality Background, by Two Major Age Categories*

| | Nationality of Mothers | | | | Nationality of Fathers | | | |
| | Under 45 Years | | 45 Years and Over | | Under 45 Years | | 45 Years and Over | |
	N	%	N	%	N	%	N	%
English, Scotch, Canadian	13	28	23	22	14	30	25	23
Irish	10	22	43	40	14	30	37	35
German	3	7	8	7	2	4	10	9
Scandinavian	3	7	4	4	2	4	4	4
Italian	1	2	3	3	1	2	3	3
Polish	2	4	2	2	3	7	3	3
Central European	2	4	–	–	2	4	–	–
Russian	–	–	2	2	–	–	1	1
Other	2	4	9	8	2	4	10	9
Undetermined	10	22	13	12	6	15	14	13
Totals[1]	46	100	107	100	46	100	107	100

[1] Negroes have been eliminated from this tabulation.

degree of ambivalence concerning the use of alcoholic beverages, ranging from the extreme antagonism reflected in the Methodist Church to the more permissive attitude of the Church of England's American counterpart, the Episcopal Church. Of crucial importance is the third factor, which involves cultural conflicts of the individual created by migration and class position. The typical offender of English extraction is a product of small-town and rural areas who is in a process of adaptation to the urban culture. Many of the adjustment problems of the Negro offender apply also to the rural-oriented lower-class white who is in a process of assimilation. For this group, in their socialization process, the culture has not blocked off the use of alcoholic beverages as a means of adaptation to stressful situations.

The Irish provide a more clear-cut case of the pervasive influence of the culture. In the United States, the Irish record a very high incidence of alcoholism compared to other groups. In the present sample, approximately 35 per cent are of Irish extraction, though the area from which the offenders are drawn is not heavily populated by the Irish. Irish rates seem to apply primarily to immigrants from rural Ireland and their lower-class descendants, since they compose the largest source of Irish-American population. The final answer to high alcohol-involvement rates of the Irish group may perhaps be found in the complex of the dependency pattern of the Irish male on his mother, which is a cultural survival from the rural Irish family (5), and in the mental set the Irishman acquires in reference to alcohol and its association with the relief of tension and anxiety (19, *p. 410*).

Table 4 reveals, furthermore, a tendency for the percentage of Irish individuals to increase in the older age category. Of offenders less than 45 years of age, 22 per cent report Irish mothers, whereas among those 45 years old and over, 40 per cent have Irish mothers; and 35 per cent of those aged 45 and over have Irish fathers, compared to 30 per cent of those under age 45. Two hypotheses seem plausibly to explain the increasing number of Irish inmates with age. First, as the social class position of the Irish in this country has improved, they are less represented in the lower social classes, and their alcoholism problems, while perhaps remaining unchanged, are now handled by clinic facilities and their own private resources. A more secure middle-class position, of course, would mean that as a group they are less subject to official police action in reference to excessive drinking. Furthermore, if Glad's (19) hypothesis that the rates apply primarily to the immigrants and their immediate descendants is correct, the decrease of Irish immigration to this country in the last 4 decades would affect the rates in a downward direction. If we assume that there are still significant numbers of Irish people in the lower social classes, which is the case, then a second hypothesis comes to the front. Chronic inebriation, since it is developmental, does not necessarily evidence itself in official police action in the earliest stages when the individual is young and possesses occupational skills that allow him to continue working while frequently drinking to excess. The Irish railroad and lakeshore workers evidence a pattern of occupational deterioration in their early 40's, which makes excessive drinking and occupational productivity incompatible. As a result, they are most subject to action by police authority, since this occupational status is associated with a lower-class position.

The situation in reference to the older Irish offender is illustrated in the following case history:

Case 1. Steven Moriarty[4] was the "baby of the family." He comes from a good church-going Irish Catholic family that resided in a Massachusetts mill town. Mr. Moriarty was a baker, and such a conscientious provider that he had little time to spend with his family. The Moriartys had seven children, but the two daughters died in childhood. Steve, the youngest, was closest to his mother and used to help her around the house

[4] All names of subjects, restaurants, hotels, and so forth, are fictional.

with the washing and household chores. Since Mr. Moriarty was always working in the bakery, Steve never shared any activities with his father.

Steve was indifferent to school work and spent all his spare time hanging around the theaters and following the "show people" around. He loved to sing and dance, and his great ambition was to be a "hoofer." This interest in the entertainment world led Steve to quit grade school before graduation. His parents accepted his decision when they found out that Steve would not return to school.

Steve was not very successful, however, in breaking into the entertainment world. His first regular employment after leaving school was a job in a cotton spinning mill, where he worked 10 hours a day for $3.60 a week in wages. This job lasted a month, after which he worked for a short time in a shoe factory. This sort of job had very little appeal for Steve, who was itching for the good times and the gay company of show people. He did not begin his wanderings, however, until after the death of his parents. Steve was 20 when his father died, and his mother died the following year. He began drinking heavily after his mother's death.

Steve went to New York and spent 5 months as a bellboy at the European Hotel. The two following seasons he worked in a resort town as a second cook and as a waiter. Although Steve now characterizes himself as an "old song and dance man, one of the best in my time," his occupational record in this regard is blank. It is doubtful that he was employed very often in this capacity, but his various jobs in hotels and restaurants evidently gave him at least the spatial proximity to the entertainment world that he desired. When Steve is asked about himself as a youth, as to his ability to make friends and his personality characteristics, he refers only to his talent as an entertainer.

From March 1918 until July 1919 Steve was in military service. He states that his drinking increased there. After his discharge he worked for over 4 years as a hospital orderly. In Maine, while working as an orderly in a Soldiers Home, he met a woman with whom he lived for 8 years. She was a "good influence" on him but refused to marry him. Steve finally left her and she later died. Steve has had no interest in women since that time.

Steve has spent short periods in shelters and railroad camps, and has received domiciliary care at several veterans homes and hospitals. In 1952 he was "booted out" of one veterans hospital because of his drinking.

Since the age of 47, when Steve was arrested 4 times for public intoxication, he has been arrested 15 times on that charge, plus once for disorderly conduct and once for vagrancy.

A year ago, when he was 62, Steve received a shoulder injury in a car accident, and this still bothers him quite a bit. He now feels that his life has been lived, that he has "had it" and has nothing left but drinking. He does not have the control to stop drinking once he starts, and his bouts last until he is jailed.

On Skid Row, which is home for the majority of the sample when they are not incarcerated, the Irish group has as its central meeting place Ma O'Conner's Cafe, which is particularly favored by the older men. The pace is relaxed and one may enjoy congregate activity which centers around stories involving Irish folklore, occupational experiences with the railroad construction crews, or products of sheer fantasy. In fact, Skid Row has numerous bars and hotels that become the center for certain cultural and racial groups.

The Italian cultural group composes between 15 and 20 per cent of the population of Monroe County, but the incarcerated sample included only four men (2 per cent) of Italian extraction. This is especially interesting because the Italian group has one of the highest rates of drinking in the United States (33). Although the Italian group in the area has begun the long climb up the social class ladder, they are primarily lower class with high vulnerability to police action—reflected in a subtle way at the Monroe County jail where instructions to visitors posted on the wall are both in English and Italian. In this particular case, social class position appears to be of little relevance in reference to public intoxication involvement, since the most important factor is the culture pattern. Due to the Italian child's early exposure to wine in the family unit, the mental set the individual acquires toward alcoholic beverages is the same as one acquires to a routine food in another cultural grouping. The individual in his socialization experiences does not come to view alcohol as a way to induce euphoria, relieve tension, reduce anxiety, or meet crises (33).

Nationality affiliation along with racial background seem to be crucial factors in determining whether a man will be involved in an alcohol problem or be incarcerated in a penal institution.

Community Background

Many laymen assume that the chronic police case inebriate is a nonresident of the community or the state in which he gives difficulty to the arresting authorities. Examination of Table 5 quickly dispels this belief. Thirteen per cent of the men were born in Monroe County, including Rochester, and 25 per cent were born in other areas of New York State. Thus, a total of 38 per cent are natives of New York State. The popular stereotype of the inebriate offender as a Negro from the South, an Irishman from Boston, or an immigrant, is by no means the complete picture. Only 9 per cent are foreign born.

TABLE 5.—*Place of Birth, by Two Major Age Categories*

	Under 45 Years		45 Years and Over		All Ages	
	N	%	N	%	N	%
Rochester and Monroe County	9	13	15	13	24	13
Rest of New York State	12	18	34	28	46	25
Elsewhere in United States	44	65	55	46	99	53
Abroad	3	4	15	13	18	9
Totals	68	100	119	100	187	100

While the majority of the offenders are nonresidents by birth, since 53 per cent were born in other states and 9 per cent abroad, this fact is congruent with the dynamics of migration in this country. The states are not closely contained demographic units but are engaged in a constant process of exporting and importing residents. A significant portion of the population growth of New York State in the last half century occurred through migration to the state, and inebriates compose one of the immigrant groups. When the sample is examined in terms of major age categories, foreign-born individuals compose 13 per cent of those aged 45 years or older, but only 4 per cent of those under 45. In the future, it may be predicted, the foreign-born will compose an insignificant proportion of the public inebriates. As indicated, the younger offenders, heavily weighted with southern Negroes, will more often be men born in other states.[5]

Monroe County is a highly urbanized center with approximately half a million residents and over 330,000 in the central city of Rochester. The county, like others in the United States, has grown both by natural increase and by the influx of new residents from small towns and rural areas of the nation which are in reality the "population seedbeds."

The sample is now an urban group, but like the general population it should include many individuals who are of rural or small-town origin. Twenty per cent of the white offenders were reared in rural areas, compared with 38 per cent of the Negro offender group. Small towns or villages of up to 25,000 inhabitants were the primary communities of 30 per cent of the whites and 24 per cent

[5] Perhaps it should not be forgotten at this juncture that New York State also exports offenders to other political jurisdictions.

of the Negroes. Approximately one-third of each group were reared in cities that ranged in size from 25,000 to 250,000, but a larger proportion of the white offenders were reared in large urban centers of over 250,000 population. When all offenders are compared by residential background, 24 per cent are rural, 29 per cent are from villages and small towns, 33 per cent are from cities of 25,000 to 250,000, and 14 per cent originated in larger urban centers.

The type of community, urban or rural, does not seem significant in this sample, unless it is viewed along with other social and cultural facts such as racial status, nationality background and social class position. Sociological studies have pointed to attitudes and cultural patterns that accompany rurality, but the most frequently utilized index of population size and density leaves the regional and class differences in rurality unaccounted for. Admittedly, the individual will experience difficulties in moving from a highly integrated folk community to a massive urban center, but the adjustment depends also upon factors of educational and occupational training, class position, and aspirations and attitudes toward urban life. Many of the rural offenders, especially lower-class whites and Negroes, have evidenced signs of inability to adapt to the highly complex urban culture, as if similar to a peasant people not geared to a machine and time-clock culture. But adaptation is further complicated by lack of educational and occupational skills and the absence of community programs that would aid in the adjustment process. The migrants from rural to urban areas are attempting to bridge the gap between two extremely different cultural systems exemplified in the prototypes of the rural South and the urban North.

Marital Status

Marriage, in human societies, is viewed as a major landmark in the cycle of experience. Within this framework, many of the societal duties and expectations referable to adult behavior are realized. The institution of marriage, with its functional bases cast in socially approved means of gratifying and regularizing the sexual impulse, in providing the nexus of procreative activities, and in forming a buttress against the forces of social and psychological aloneness, is also an extremely demanding institution. A successful marriage is built around competences developed in interpersonal relationships over the socialization cycle. Some individuals never enter into the marriage relationship or, once involved, are unable to develop a

TABLE 6.—*Marital Status of the Sample Compared to the General Population*

| | General Population[1] | | Sample | |
	N	%	N	%
Single	31,465	25.5	77	41
Married, wife present	78,720	63.9	4	2
Married, wife absent	4,700	3.8	59	32
Widowed	6,580	5.3	35	6
Divorced	1,800	1.5	12	19
Totals	141,710	100.0	187	100

[1] Males aged 14 years and over residing in the Rochester Standard Metropolitan area, which encompasses the same area as Monroe County, New York. Source: 1950 United States Census of Population, "New York: Detailed Characteristics," Bulletin PC–32, Table 57, pp. 32–206.

satisfactory adjustment to marital situations. This may be but is not always expressed in a separated or divorced status.

The marital status of the sample is compared in Table 6 to that of the male population aged 14 years and over in 1950 in the Rochester Standard Metropolitan Area. Apparently 41 per cent of the inebriates had never married, compared to 25.5 per cent of the Rochester area male population. In addition, about 12 times as many of the inebriates have been divorced. The same trend is evidenced in separations without divorce, experienced by approximately 8 times as many inebriates. Finally, only 2 per cent of the inebriates were married and living with their spouses, compared to some 64 per cent of the general population, which includes many below the usual age of marriage.

Perhaps the situation in reference to marital status is placed in better perspective in Table 7, which reports the observed and expected marital status distribution of the penitentiary inebriates by age categories. At all age levels there is a higher percentage of single men than would be expected from the marital status distribution of the general population of the Rochester Standard Metro-

TABLE 7.—*Observed and Expected[1] Marital Status, by Age Categories (in Per Cent)*

| | Under 35 | | 35–44 | | 45–54 | | 55 and Over | |
	Obs.	Exp.	Obs.	Exp.	Obs.	Exp.	Obs.	Exp.
Single	58	46	29	11	48	9	37	9
Married, wife present	5	51	6	83	0	82	0	70
Married, wife absent	16	2	41	3	28	4	33	4
Widowed	0	0	6	1	3	3	14	16
Divorced	21	1	18	2	21	2	16	1

[1] Expected marital status was computed from the marital distribution of the male population over 14 years of age in the Rochester Standard Metropolitan Area in 1950.

politan Area, which is used as the control. The same observation holds for the separated and divorced categories. Among the offenders aged 45 years or older, there is not one intact marriage relationship. This stands in startling contrast to the fact that in the general population of the county 82 per cent of men aged 45 to 54 and 70 per cent of those aged 55 and over are living with their spouses. Thus, when analyzed by age categories, the fact of the large proportion of these inebriates who never entered the marriage relationship, or who once entered but were unable to maintain it, emerges in its full dramatic impact.

Table 8 presents a summary of the marital status reported in four groups of problem drinkers. Among the penitentiary inebriates, 41 per cent had never married, compared to 56 per cent of the men interviewed in a New Haven shelter by Straus (46) and 53 per cent of men arrested for public intoxication in Connecticut in 1942 (3). This discrepancy can be explained by the fact that both of the latter samples had a higher percentage expectancy of single status than the present sample. Factors of time differences in the studies, as well as chance, may also be involved. But the fact remains that in all three groups the percentage of single men is much higher than expected in the general populations used as controls. Only in the alcoholic patients who were seen in alcoholism clinics (49) did the proportion who were single equal expectancy.

But marriage per se does not mean that success has been achieved in the handling of this most crucial interpersonal relationship in the society. Table 8 reveals that of individuals in the homeless man group in New Haven who attempted marriage, 99 per cent reported the marriages broken by divorce, separation or death, whereas the normal expectancy, using the general population as the control, would have been 12 per cent. The present study group of peni-

TABLE 8.—*Observed and Expected Marital Status of Four Groups of Problem Drinkers* (*in Per Cent*)

	Percentage Never Married		Percentage of Those Married Who were Ever Separated, Divorced or Widowed	
	Observed	*Expected*	*Observed*	*Expected*
Present sample	41	13	96	11
Clinic patients[1]	20	21	36	9
Homeless men[1]	56	15	99	12
Arrested inebriates[1]	53	20	51	11

[1] Source: Straus and Bacon (49, p. 239).

tentiary inmates is the most nearly comparable in that 96 per cent
of those who had ever married reported broken marriages, whereas
the expectancy is only 11 per cent, using the general male population of Monroe County, corrected for age disparities, as the control.
Less extreme is the record of the arrested Connecticut inebriates
who reported 51 per cent of the marriages broken when the expected percentage was 11; and still less that of patients seen in
alcoholism clinics, whose observed rate of 36 per cent broken marriages compares with an expected rate of 9 per cent.

What conclusions can be drawn from these four studies? Alcoholism clinic patients show the same propensity to marry as the
general population, which is not true of the homeless men, the arrested inebriates, and the chronic police case inebriates. The marriages of all these groups evidence the same trend toward marked
instability. Marriage instability is most marked among the homeless
men and the chronic police case inebriates, who have generally
reached the bottom of the social escalator and are no longer completely functioning members of the society or the community. The
middle point is occupied by arrested inebriates, who still evidence
certain signs of social stability, but these characteristics of integration are not as high as those of patients seen in alcoholism clinics,
whose marriage stability rate is the highest. Marital status, of course,
is only one indication, but still an extremely important index, of
social integration. The relationship which exists between marriage
stability and problem drinking is a complex one. Many individuals
do not possess the competences in interpersonal relations or in personality traits that are associated with entrance into marriage; or,
once involved in marriage, these individuals do not possess the
requisite skills for continuing the marriage. Excessive drinking,
which eventually causes disruptions in all areas of the social life
space of the individual, is destructive of the marriage relationship
itself (29). As the drinking behavior becomes more intense, it con-
sumes more and more of the physical, psychological and social energy which is needed for the performance of tasks in other areas
of the life space, such as the marriage relationship. In the final
phases of alcoholism the expenditure of energy by the individual
is almost completely devoted to a gratification of the need to drink
(26). The intensity of the relationship between the late stage alcoholic and alcohol precludes the formation or continuance of other
relationships which are potential drainers of energy.

Educational Attainment

Education in all societies is more than the formal learning by the individual of specific facts and techniques related to subject matter, such as chemistry. It is also preparation for living, and creates the situation in which the development of human potentialities can take place. When the child enters the educational institution, the socialization process continues in a wider setting than hitherto, when only the family and play group were involved. He must learn new rules and regulations, assume new duties and obligations, and extend the range of significant others in the environment to whom he must adjust and with whom he can form interpersonal bonds. Many of the roles which he must assume in adult society can be experimented with in their elementary forms in the school situation. Thus the social situations and groupings in the educational institution provide a crucial setting in which the personality development and group adaptation of the individual occur.

On a more formal plane, exposure to and achievement of the subject matter presented in the school allow the individual to obtain skills with which he is able to manipulate all phases of his environment. Formal educational achievement is still one of the foremost means by which upward social mobility, with its consequent financial rewards and social recognition, is obtained. In short, the possession of educational skills allows the individual a wider latitude in charting his social life space. Nonattainment of educational skills handicaps the individual in many ways: He is never maximally exposed to the informal and formal learning situations which would aid him in his adult placement in society; he never fully experiences the socialization processes that are concurrent particularly with education; and he may be barred from a variety of contacts in the economic sphere.

The men in the present sample represent a particularly disadvantaged group when analyzed in terms of formal schooling. In Table 9 they are compared to two groups: the general population of all males over 24 years of age in Monroe County, and a group of men arrested for public intoxication in Connecticut in 1942. It can be seen that approximately the same proportion of the general population and the incarcerated inebriates enter school, but the retaining power of the educational institutions was less for the future inebriates. Of the chronic police case sample, 70 per cent terminated their schooling by the end of grammar school, compared to 40 per

TABLE 9.—*Educational Attainment of the Sample Compared with the General Population and a Group Arrested for Intoxication in Connecticut (in Per Cent)*

	General Population[1]	Arrested Inebriates[2]	Present Sample
No schooling	2.6	5.7	3.0
Part grade school	18.8	36.1	38.0
Completed grade school	20.2	32.3	32.0
Part high school	19.7	13.4	13.0
Completed high school	20.5	7.1	10.0
Part college	6.3	3.1	3.0
Completed college or more	8.8	2.3	0.5
Undetermined	3.1	0	0.5
Totals	*100.0*	*100.0*	*100.0*

[1] All males over 24 years of age in the Rochester Standard Metropolitan Area in 1950. Source: 1950 United States Census of Population, "New York: Detailed Characteristics," Bulletin PB–32, Table 34, pp. 32–90.

[2] Source: Bacon (3, p. 36).

cent in the general population. Moving progressively up the educational ladder, the differences in educational attainment become greater, reaching a peak in terms of completion of college, which 8.8 per cent of the general population achieved, compared to only 0.5 per cent of the incarcerated inebriates. It seems noteworthy that the latter show the same general educational attainment as do the people arrested for drunkenness investigated by Bacon (3).

The discrepancy between the educational attainment of both groups of inebriates and the general population can perhaps be explained in terms of the operation of social class factors. The inebriates are primarily individuals who were originally of lower-middle position or lower in the social class order; they have the highest vulnerability to arrest; they are, moreover, a "declassed" group, moving downward in the society.

Occupational Status

The occupational status of an individual serves as one major index of his placement in the economic and social order of a community. Furthermore, the financial rewards which are built into the occupational positions will determine the kinds, quality and number of material objects available to the individual. Occupations are ranged in a hierarchy from those of low esteem and few rewards to those of high esteem and many rewards. Thus, occupation is an important point of reference around which centers the ranking

TABLE 10.—*Primary Occupational Skills of the Sample Compared to Occupational Status of the General Population (in Per Cent)*

	Present Sample	General Population[1]
Professional, technical, managers and proprietors*	3	22
Clerical and kindred, sales workers*	2	14
Skilled workers*	22	46
Unskilled workers*	68	13
Other and unknown	5	5

[1] All males 14 years of age and over in the labor force in the Rochester Standard Metropolitan Area in 1950. Source: 1950 United States Census of Population, "New York: Detailed Characteristics," Bulletin PB–32, Table 35, pp. 32–100.

* Difference is statistically significant at the .01 level.

of individuals and their access to rights and privileges in the society.

In studying the chronic police case inebriate, first attention was given to the individual's primary occupational skills, regardless of whether they were currently being utilized. An occupational classification of four groups was adopted for simplicity: (a) professional and allied; (b) clerical and sales; (c) skilled; and (d) unskilled. In Table 10 a comparison is presented of the primary occupational skills of the men in the sample with the occupational classification of males in the Rochester area 14 years of age or over, designated as the general population. It can be seen that even in terms of primary occupational skills the former reflect a significantly different pattern than do the general population. The overwhelming concentration of inebriates, 68 per cent, is found in the unskilled category, compared to 13 per cent of the general population; 22 per cent of the inebriates are primarily in the category of skilled workers, compared to 46 per cent of the general population. The widest discrepancies occur in the highly esteemed category of professional and allied workers, which includes 22 per cent of the general population but only 3 per cent of the inebriates; and in the clerical and sales category where the ratio is seven of the general population to one of the inebriates. All of these differences are statistically significant at the .01 level.

Thus, the primary occupational skills of the inebriates are skewed toward the bottom of the economic hierarchy, toward those jobs which evoke the least esteem in the culture and provide the least remuneration. It must be remembered, however, that we have considered primary skills and not present job classifications. Here some distortion undoubtedly enters the assessment of the economic position of these men, since many of them have not been gainfully employed at their primary skill for many years but rather have been engaged in a downward spiral.

The low order of occupational resources and skills possessed by the chronic police case inebriate fits into the general syndrome of factors which are emerging concerning this individual. Marked by low educational attainment, from disadvantaged social groups in the society, and lacking in occupational skills, his adaptation level seems destined to be marginal in the society.

Religious Affiliation

The chronic police case inebriates may be characterized also in terms of their religious background. The effect of religious orientation and affiliation on behavior is extremely difficult to judge with accuracy, owing to extreme variations in the intensity of belief, which is the chief determinant of the role that religion may play in the life activities of the individual. However, most members of society are accorded a religious affiliation at birth, even though the parents may make no formal identification with a church. In general, the religious group provides the individual with a frame of reference for viewing the universe and social reality and the system of beliefs may provide psychological mechanisms for the relief of guilt and anxieties, thereby promoting mental well-being. But merely nominal affiliation does not mean that the individual will consciously identify with the system of belief. Thus, information on religious affiliation may aid in predicting the individual's behavior, but other variables such as the intensity of belief and the role of the religious ideas in the total personality of the individual are more crucial than the bare sociological fact.

With this reservation in view, the religious affiliation of the incarcerated inebriates can be examined and its significance can be discussed. Table 11 presents the religious affiliations of the sample

TABLE 11.—*Religious Affiliation, by Age Categories (in Per Cent)*

Age (years)	Protestant	Catholic	None
Under 35	74*	5*	21
35–44	39	39	22
45–54	37	47	16
55 and over	40	43	17
Totals	*42*	*40*	*18*

* Difference between the age categories under 35 and 35 or older is statistically significant, at the .01 level, for the Catholic–Protestant portion of the offenders.

by age categories. No attempt has been made to utilize a control group from the general population, for several reasons. First, the Census does not record the religious affiliation of individuals as it does other relevant general characteristics of the population. Second, the data published by several religious bodies in the United States are not suitable for comparison, since different age limits are used by various churches in determining membership, and there is a lack of uniformity and accuracy in recording affiliation. Furthermore, the particular religious distribution of the inebriates may reflect only local or unique factors. In the present sample, 42 per cent reported themselves as Protestants, 40 per cent as Catholics, and 18 per cent as without any religious affiliation. There were no Jews in the sample. An examination of the cases of the 18 per cent reporting no religious affiliation reveals no evidence that these men had any Jewish identification.

The most significant factor in this religious distribution is the absence of Jews. Other studies in the field of alcoholism have noted the low vulnerability of Jews to involvement in excessive drinking behavior and their low rates of alcoholism. Hyde and Chisholm reported that selective service rejection rates for neuropsychiatric disorders during the Second World War were higher among Jews than among Irish. But alcoholism accounted for only 0.2 per cent of the rejections of Jews for neuropsychiatric disorders, compared to 3 per cent of the Irish rejections.[6] This becomes increasingly significant in the light of the fact that in a nationwide sample studied by Riley and Marden (42) it was found that 59 per cent of the Protestants, 79 per cent of the Catholics, and 87 per cent of the Jews were users of alcoholic beverages. Thus the problem drinker does not come from the religious group which has the highest incidence of drinking. The low rates of alcoholism among Jews and their absence from an institutional population jailed for excessive drinking may be explicable in terms of the cultural norms which define the perception that Jews obtain of alcohol during the socialization process and the ritual significance attached to wine in the Jewish family, as Bales (5) and Snyder (45) have suggested.

When the religious affiliation of the inebriates is examined (Table 11) by age categories, it is seen that a statistically significant differ-

[6] Cited from Glad (19, *p. 408*). See also the extensive discussion and review of statistical reports on the low incidence of "alcohol pathologies" among the Jews by Snyder (45).

ence exists in the Catholic–Protestant proportion among those who are less than 35 years of age. In this most youthful portion of the sample 74 per cent are Protestants, 5 per cent are Catholics, and 21 per cent are not religiously affiliated. The high proportion of Protestants is derived from the fact that approximately half the men in this age category are Negroes, and in American society Negroes are chiefly affiliated with Protestant churches. The Irish, who form the highest concentration of Catholics in the sample, enter the institution at a later age period, as has been observed earlier. However, alcoholism rates in the predominantly Catholic Italians are low. This fact would indicate that the more crucial factor in reference to drinking behavior, with the exception of Jews who are both a cultural and religious group, is one of membership in a particular cultural or nationality group and not religious affiliation.

Residential Mobility

The residential mobility pattern of the chronic police case inebriate serves as another criterion by which the group may be characterized. It is commonly assumed that residential stability, along with steady employment and an unbroken marriage relationship, are indices of the social stability and integration of the individual in the larger community and also on the personal level. Why is this assumption made concerning residential stability?

It is obvious that residential mobility cannot be viewed in an entirely negative light. Mobility can be productive of skills in interpersonal relations and in coping with different kinds of interaction. It can provide the nexus around which the individual meets more social situations. Theoretically the level of personality adaptation of the geographically mobile individual may excel that of the non-mobile one whose contacts with social situations are of a stereotyped and routine variety. But there are also dysfunctions involved in excessive mobility, both on the societal and personal level. Excessive mobility may result in lack of identification with a neighborhood or a larger community where the individual is able to sink his taproots down into the fertile soil of social control, of rules, norms and expectancies of behavior from which he will draw the rewards and punishments for his behavior. To assume, however, that the chronic police case inebriates are completely without community roots would be fallacious. It is more in accord with observed facts to assume that their present personal and community identification is with the subcommunity of Skid Row whose norms and values are not the same as those of the larger society or community. A stereotyped comment concerning the inebriate in a penal institution or on Skid Row is that he has "resigned from society." This statement makes the dubious assumption that the individual was at one time a member of the larger society, acting in full accord with its norms and values, and that at some point in his life career he resigned. A much more plausible theory, in view of the social characteristics thus far presented, is that he was never a member of the larger society as it is framed in the middle-class sense, and consequently has seldom been in harmony with that society. Instead, his level of adaptation and focus of identification are to be found in other levels of society, such as Skid Row or the penal institution, which are qualitatively different from the larger society.

That this group does possess a degree of residential stability is discerned in Table 12 which presents the length of residence of the incarcerated inmates in New York State and Monroe County. For example, 37 per cent of the men are natives of New York, and 13 per cent were born in Monroe County. It may be assumed that 5 or more years of residence in one community is indicative of stability; 62 per cent of these men have been in Rochester and its environs that long. If 3 or more years of continuous residence is taken as the criterion of average stability, then 69 per cent of the men are in this category. On the other hand, hardly 8 per cent have resided less than a year in New York State, and the comparable statistic for Monroe County is 15 per cent. It is assumed, however, that these findings represent a higher degree of instability than would be

TABLE 12.—*Length of Residence in New York State and Monroe County* (*in Per Cent*)

	New York State		Monroe County	
	N	%	N	%
Less than 6 months	6	3.2	18	9.7
6 months to a year	8	4.3	9	4.8
1–3 years	24	12.8	31	16.7
3–5 years	13	6.9	12	6.4
5 or more years	66	35.4	92	49.5
Born in and permanent	70	37.4	24	12.9
Totals	*187*	*100.0*	*186*[1]	*100.0*

[1] One case omitted because this information is lacking.

found in the general population if such data were available by age-corrected categories.

A further indication of the degree of community stability can be gathered from the number of communities in which the incarcerated inebriates have lived during the past 2 years. Of those under 45 years old, 53 per cent had lived only in the Rochester community, compared to 69 per cent of those 45 years of age and over. This may represent a slightly higher degree of community stability in the older men. Straus and Bacon (49, *p. 241*), however, found in their study of alcoholism clinic patients that 89 per cent had resided in the reported town of residence more than 2 years, compared to 63 per cent of the present sample. Thus, the chronic police case inebriates show less community stability than the clinic patients.

Another index of the residential stability of this group is the number of places of residence during the previous 2 years. By this criterion the inebriates are a highly mobile group, moving at frequent intervals from place to place. Thus 23 per cent reported one or two residences during the previous 2 years, 23 per cent from three to five, and 54 per cent six or more residences. It should be noted, however, that the residential mobility is of the intracommunity variety rather than intercommunity.

Finally, the residential instability of the chronic police case inebriates is reflected in the type of residence reported at arrest. This is shown in Table 13, and compared with the residential status of patients seen in alcoholism clinics throughout the country. At the time of their arrest, 39 per cent of the present sample had no

TABLE 13.—*Type of Residence of the Sample at Time of Arrest Compared with Alcoholism Clinic Patients (in Per Cent)*

	Present Sample	Clinic Patients[1]
No permanent residence[2]	38.7	0
Mission or shelter	11.3	4.0
Living on job	4.3	1.0
Hotel or rooming house	34.4	16.0
Home of relatives or friends	5.9	23.0
Own home or apartment	5.4	55.0
Hospitals, jails	0	1.0
Totals	*100.0*	*100.0*

[1] Source: Straus and Bacon (49, p. 240).

[2] The high percentage of "no permanent residence" reflects the fact that residence in Skid Row "flophouses" is so recorded, and the further factor that many of these men are rearrested after release from the penal institution before they take up residence anywhere.

permanent residence, compared to none of the clinic patients. This finding is explained by the fact that many of the former were living in "flophouses," where a bed is paid for nightly, or had very recently been released from jail and were apprehended again by the police before they had achieved some degree of residential permanency. The fact is, however, that almost 40 per cent of these men had no residential identification even with a public shelter or a cheap hotel, and preferred to state they lived from place to place. Other types of residence indicative of social instability were also reported more frequently by the chronic police case inebriates than the clinic patients. Only 6 per cent of the former reported residence with friends or relatives, compared to 23 per cent of the clinic patients. Probably the most significant factor is that fewer than 6 per cent of the incarcerated inebriates were living in their own home or apartment, compared to 55 per cent of the clinic group.

In summary, the incarcerated inebriate evidences marked residential instability in terms of changes in place of residence within the community and type of residence when arrested, but a moderate degree of stability in terms of length of residence in the state and community and number of communities of residence during the previous 2 years.

Criminal History

The chronic police case inebriates as a category can be further distinguished in terms of their experiences with constituted authority as reflected in the arresting and incarceration process. Students of social class, such as Warner (63) and Hollingshead (24), have pointed out in their empirical studies of communities that arrest and incarceration are phenomena alien to middle or upper-class position in a society and would be viewed by these classes with shame and abhorrence if either occurred to a member. Lower-class groups, on the contrary, are particularly vulnerable to arrest and incarceration in our society, and exposure to jailing is recorded in the folk music which appeals to lower-class groups in such songs as the recent "I'm in the Jailhouse Now" and the older "Birmingham Jail." Thus the music as well as other facets of the culture inform the observer that the lower class has had experience with the process of jailing and arrest. But the society as a whole views the person who is arrested and incarcerated for any offense in a negative light, since this is a violation of the values that center around middle-class respectability.

On the cultural front, the individual who is constantly arrested and imprisoned has a stigma attached to him by the rest of society and is outside the pale of respectability. But as crucial as the cultural values, which define the responses of the class groups to arrest and incarceration, is the psychological impact of these two events on the individual who experiences them. It may be argued with logic that an isolated arrest without incarceration may have little influence on the personality, and this is perhaps the case. But the psychological impact of a continual process of arrest and incarceration on the individual and on his self-conception are of a different order. Imprisonment, which occurs in American society in a framework of repression, authoritarianism and rigidity, is not conducive to the development of initiative and maturity in the individual. The effects are perhaps more severe in the individuals who have committed only nuisance offenses such as public intoxication and vagrancy and whose behavior in many cases is symptomatic of an illness or disturbance in the personality. Whatever be the value of this belief, the fact remains that society's accepted manner of dealing with the public drunkard is to place him in a county or city jail or penitentiary, along with other misdemeanants, where the framework is one of repression instead of treatment. In the process, the resources of the individual suffer further deterioration and the development of the institutionalized offender occurs— one whose pattern of life becomes a constant movement from incarceration to release and reincarceration, with increasing dependency on the institution.

The extent to which this revolving-door policy for the chronic inebriate is in operation can be discerned from a detailed examination of the criminal histories of the sample. These histories were obtained from the arrest and incarceration records of each offender as maintained by the county penal authorities. Admittedly these records are not accurate in all respects; like all criminal statistics they suffer from lack of reliability in reference to recording and ambiguity in the behavioral categories. Nevertheless these records do furnish a general picture of the minimum number and types of arrests which these men have experienced during their life careers.

Table 14 summarizes by four age categories the lifetime arrest experience of the chronic police case inebriates. For the group

TABLE 14.—*Recorded Arrests for All Offenses, by Age Categories*

Frequency of Arrests	Under 35		35–44		45–54		55 and Over		All Ages	
	N	%	N	%	N	%	N	%	N	%
2–5	12	63.2	13	26.5	11	16.2	10	20.0	46	24.6
6–9	2	10.5	12	24.5	12	17.7	12	24.0	38	20.4
10–19	5	26.3	15	30.6	27	39.6	8	16.0	55	29.5
20–39	0	0	8	16.3	9	13.3	11	22.0	28	15.1
40 and over	0	0	1	2.1	9	13.2	9	18.0	19	10.4
Mean		6.8		11.6		18.1		22.9		16.5
Median		4.0		9.0		12.0		13.0		10.2
Total Cases	19	100.0	49	100.0	68	100.0	50	100.0	186	100.0
Total Arrests	129		571		1,234		1,144		3,078	

as a whole, a total of 3,078 arrests were recorded for all offense categories ranging from criminal homicide to vagrancy. The individual number of arrests ranged from 2 in 10 cases to the extreme of 110 arrests in one case. The mean frequency of arrests was 16.5, and the median for the entire group, 10.2. When the data are examined in terms of age categories, a significant though not unexpected finding emerges. The number of arrests increases progressively with increase in age. The mean number of arrests for offenders less than 35 years of age was 6.8, with a median of 4.0; for offenders aged 35 to 44 years, the mean was 11.6 and the median 9.0; for offenders aged 45 to 54, the mean was 18.1 and the median 12.0; while for the oldest group, aged 55 years or more, the mean number of arrests was 22.9 and the median 13.0. The difference in the medians between the two oldest categories, however, is only 1. The difference in the means between these two groups is due to the presence of a larger number of the extreme cases (in terms of number of arrests) in the oldest category. Despite the increasing number of arrests related to increasing age, it should be noted that in the two older age brackets there are individuals who have had the minimum number of incarcerations to meet the sample criterion, and this evidences the fact that arrests and incarcerations for certain problem drinkers may be phenomena of later life, when all other props have been removed and complete deterioration of resources has occurred. In the younger age groups, those under 45, the pattern of excessive arrest and incarceration has already established itself; this is revealed by the fact that approximately 85 per cent of them have been arrested or incarcerated four or more times.

In this investigation the focus is on the public inebriate who has been a problem to the constituted sources of authority; we are therefore especially concerned with the extent of public intoxication as viewed from the arrest records. Public intoxication was responsible for 2,387 arrests of the sample and accounted for 77.5 per cent of all their recorded arrests. This record, however, definitely underrepresents the number of arrests involving the excessive use of alcohol, since in many jurisdictions the individual is booked on a charge other than public intoxication, e.g., disorderly conduct or vagrancy. But since there is no accurate means of assessing this factor, the official record must suffice for the present analysis.

Table 15 presents a frequency distribution of the arrests of the men in the sample for public intoxication, by the age categories. For all age groups combined the mean number of arrests is 12.8, with a median of 6.0. It is of interest to note that Bacon (3, p. 4), in his survey of individuals arrested for intoxication in Connecticut in 1942, found the same median. The age category reveals a trend for the mean and median number of arrests to increase with age. For the offenders less than 35 years of age, the mean number of arrests is 4.1 with a median of 2.3; for those between 35 and 44 years of age, the mean is 8.2 and the median 5.3; for those aged between 45 and 54, the mean is 14.4 and the median 8.3; and for those 55 years of age or older, the mean is 18.6 with a median of 9.0. Again the difference between the medians of the two upper age categories is small.

Substantial differences exist also in the range of the number of

TABLE 15.—*Recorded Arrests for Public Intoxication, by Age Categories*

Frequency of Arrests	Under 35		35–44		45–54		55 and Over		All Ages	
	N	%	N	%	N	%	N	%	N	%
2–5	15	78.9	24	48.9	21	30.9	18	36.0	78	41.9
6–9	3	15.8	12	24.5	17	24.9	7	14.0	39	21.0
10–19	1	5.3	9	18.4	14	20.5	8	16.0	32	17.2
20–39	0	0	3	6.1	9	13.3	11	22.0	23	12.3
40 and over	0	0	1	2.1	7	10.4	6	12.0	14	7.6
Mean		4.1		8.2		14.4		18.6		12.8
Median		2.3		5.3		8.3		9.0		6.0
Total Cases	19	100.0	49	100.0	68	100.0	50	100.0	186	100.0
Total Arrests	78		404		977		928		2,387	

arrests for public intoxication. The range of the entire sample is from 2 to 110 arrests, but the widest ranges are in the two upper age categories. For those 55 and over the range is from 2 arrests to 110, but with the concentration in the frequency categories of less than 10 arrests. The same is true of the men in the 45 to 54 age bracket, which shows a range of 2 to 72 arrests. In the younger age brackets the ranges are much smaller: from 2 to 19 arrests in those under 35, and from 2 to 40 in those aged 35 to 44. From this analysis it appears that the offender who is marked by 30 or 40 or more arrests for public intoxication is atypical, and that the typical chronic police case inebriate has experienced fewer than 10 arrests on this particular charge.

As has been noted previously, 22.5 per cent of the arrests experienced by these men are on charges other than public intoxication. The mean number of arrests on other charges is 3.7, with a median of 2.0. When analyzed by age categories, the pattern of increase with age observed in public intoxication arrests does not hold true for other charges. For those under age 35, the mean number of arrests on other charges is 2.7, the median 1.0; for those aged 35 to 44, the mean is 3.4 and the median 2.0; for those aged 45 to 54, the mean is 3.8 and the median 2.0; and for those aged 55 years and older, the mean is 4.3 and the median 2.1. On the whole, the number of arrests on charges other than public intoxication does not show a significant increase with aging after 35. This is reflected in the medians of the groups, although the means do increase slightly because of a subgroup of men whose offenses increase continually with age, resulting in a distortion of the total picture. It is suspected that the increase in means with increasing age would be less if each bout with alcohol were accurately recorded as public intoxication instead of disorderly conduct or vagrancy. The explanation for the failure of other offenses to increase with age lies in the fact that at the end of the first utilized age period, 35, there is a trend for the inebriates who have been involved in more serious crimes, such as automobile theft or burglary, to cease this type of criminal activity, and for the intoxication pattern of behavior to emerge as an adaptation to the life situation.

It should be noted that 31 per cent of the offenders (58 cases) have never been arrested on any charge other than public intoxication. But the full meaning of this statistic cannot be discerned until an examination is made of the types of "other" offenses committed by the inebriates and their frequency. These data are presented in Table 16.

As is indicated in Table 16, the men in this sample have been arrested for a variety of offenses in their careers, ranging from the least frequent categories of gambling and criminal homicide to the more frequent one of vagrancy, for which they have a recorded 175 arrests. Following this in terms of frequency are 106 arrests for disorderly conduct, and the same number for larceny, 48 for "aggravated assault" and 41 for burglary. It is interesting that these 187 chronic inebriates have among them experienced only 22 arrests for driving while intoxicated. In addition, they have recorded 100 arrests on a variety of miscellaneous charges such as trespassing and begging.

The statistics of arrest for offenses other than public intoxication raise certain pertinent questions concerning the behavioral differences which can be attributed to these categories. That these offense categories on the whole are not qualitatively the same is obvious, but of what relevance are they for the behavior of the inebriate?

We can divide the other offense categories into two groups: those which appear to be related to the problems that are engen-

TABLE 16.—*Distribution of Arrests for Other Offenses than Public Intoxication*

	Frequency	Number of Offenders	Percentage of All Offenders
Criminal homicide	2	2	1.1
Rape	5	4	2.2
Robbery	14	11	5.9
Burglary	41	24	12.8
Larceny	106	44	23.5
Car theft	10	7	3.8
Forgery, counterfeiting	6	5	2.7
Embezzlement, fraud	6	3	1.6
Carrying and possessing weapons	8	8	4.3
Offenses involving family and children	19	13	7.0
Narcotics law violations	12	6	3.2
Liquor law violations	9	2	1.1
Gambling	2	1	0.6
Aggravated assault	48	24	12.8
Disorderly conduct	106	41	22.0
Vagrancy	175	66	35.5
Driving while intoxicated	22	14	7.5
All other offenses	100	51	27.4
Total	*691*		

dered by excessive drinking, and those that seem to bear little relationship to drinking behavior in general. The offenses which appear to be closely associated with problems of chronic inebriation, and which at times may be the official way of recording drunken behavior, are vagrancy, which becomes a high risk category in the inebriate's excessive mobility and lack of steady employment, and disorderly conduct, which may be the charge used instead of public intoxication by the arresting officials. The same situation may prevail in the case of aggravated assault, which may happen during the drinking bout. The married inebriate also tends to have problems with his family and children, particularly in reference to financial support. The offense categories of liquor law violations, driving while intoxicated, gambling, and the carrying and possessing of weapons have been assumed by some to be alcohol-related offenses, too. But whether these offense categories bear a closer relationship to public intoxication than do certain others, is very uncertain, and for that reason they have not been grouped with the public intoxication cases. In all, 59 of the men, 32 per cent of the sample, have been arrested not only for public intoxication but also for driving while intoxicated, vagrancy, disorderly conduct, aggravated assault, gambling, violation of liquor laws, offenses involving family and children, carrying and possessing weapons, or for one of the miscellaneous offenses designated "other" in Table 16.

A substantial number of the incarcerated inebriates, however, have more serious criminal arrest records from the viewpoint of society as reflected by their arrest and conviction on felony charges which appear to have less relationship to the problem of excessive drinking. This group is comprised of 69 men, 37 per cent of the sample, who have been charged with criminal homicide, rape, robbery, burglary, larceny, automobile theft, forgery, counterfeiting, embezzlement, fraud, narcotics law violations. Table 16 reveals that almost one-fourth of the sample have been arrested for grand or petit larceny, 1 out of 8 has been arrested for burglary, 1 out of 20 for robbery, and 1 out of 25 for automobile theft. Many of these offenses may have been committed under the influence of alcohol, yet the overwhelming majority of drinkers in general and inebriates in particular do not commit these acts under the same influence. The search for causation must delve deeper into the personality than noting that a man was inebriated when the act occurred. However, the finding that over one-third of the incarcerated inebriates have had ordinary criminal careers which were unsuccessful lends some support to the belief, hitherto unsupported by empirical fact, that a significant portion of the population incarcerated for public intoxication has spent time in state and federal correctional institutions, and that the pattern of excessive drinking is an adaptation to the lack of success in the criminal career.

One more conclusion can be drawn concerning this group of primarily felony violators. Examination of their arrest records reveals that the criminal career is generally divided into two distinct phases. The first covers the earlier years of life, generally when the man is under 40 years of age, and is marked by arrests and incarcerations for offenses that are seemingly unrelated to excessive use of alcohol. But these arrests and incarcerations mean that their attempted criminal careers have been unsuccessful. They then drop out of active crime, not only because of ineptness and age, but also through the emergence of the new pattern of adaptation to societal norms and requirements which is reflected in increased drinking and life on Skid Row. In terms of their perception of the life situation, drinking forms a part of a new pattern of gratifying psychological needs, replacing the unsuccessful attempt to achieve that gratification in a career of crimes against property. However, this phasic pattern is neither rigid nor universal, since arrests and convictions for public intoxication do occur earlier in many histories, though not in great frequency. This pattern can perhaps best be demonstrated by the brief case history of one of the men in the sample.

Case 2. Howard Raymond, at present 66 years old, characterizes himself as a "worn-out drunk," but there is more to his history than that. At the age of 14 he was committed to an institution for juvenile delinquents in New York State for a series of thefts in his home town. At this reformatory, he states, he "learned a lot" which aided him in his later career, which is punctuated by numerous incarcerations in penal institutions. A chronological review of his criminal career would reveal the following history:

At the age of 14 he was sentenced to a juvenile reformatory for theft. He was paroled, violated parole, was returned to the institution and paroled again. At 19 he was incarcerated in the state reformatory for theft, and while on parole from this institution was sentenced to the state prison for rape. Again he was paroled, violated the conditions, and was returned to prison. At 28, because of his frequent violations of parole and a grand larceny offense, he was sentenced to an indeterminate term in prison. At 30 he was released from prison to join the Army, but he spent most of his time in the detention barracks for absence without leave, insubordination, and breaking arrest. He was given a dishonorable discharge from the Army. At 35 he was committed to the state prison after a conviction for grand larceny. He was released on parole. At 40, convicted of assault, he was once again sentenced to prison, this time for the rest of his natural life, but after 7 years his case was reviewed and he was paroled.

In the 19 years since then his record has been free of any major infractions of the criminal code, but the significant point to note is that arrests for public intoxication, formerly isolated and infrequent in his arrest history, now show an increase in frequency. From the age of 47 to his present age of 66 his record shows more than 45 arrests for public intoxication. As far as society is concerned, Howard Raymond is no longer a serious problem in terms of the type of the offense he commits. He has drifted into a drinking pattern which may be viewed as an adaptation in substitution for his previous unsuccessful career in crime.

The case of Howard Raymond, though extreme in terms of its criminal history, amply illustrates the phasic quality of the career pattern. The early career in crime was unsuccessful and covered the first decades in the individual's attempted adjustment. The later pattern, which may have been foreshadowed in the earlier drinking history, is a rapid involvement in the pattern of public intoxication as an adaptation to the individual's disorganized life situation.

The chronic police case inebriates are, in reality, a heterogeneous category in respect to their criminal behavior as reflected in their arrest records. This is true on two scores. First, there are wide variations in the number of times they have become involved with constituted authority as reflected in arrest and incarceration records. It is worth reemphasizing, however, that the stereotyped picture of a man with 30 or 40 or more arrests and incarcerations is not an accurate statistical portrayal of the group, though many individuals in the sample reflect this attribute of frequent incarceration. Second, there are wide variations in criminal experience. There appear to be, indeed, 3 major subgroupings in reference to criminal records. One subgroup is composed of 58 men (31 per cent of the sample) who have never been arrested on any charge other than public intoxication; a second is composed of 59 men (32 per cent) who have been arrested not only for public intoxication but on charges which are probably associated with excessive use of alcohol, or on charges of a minor nature; and a third is composed of 69 men (37 per cent) who not only are chronic police case inebriates but have been involved in serious violations of the legal norms of the society, such as felony offenses.

At this point, however, a word of caution concerning the reliability of criminal arrest records must be entered. Criminologists have long been aware that many more violations of the legal norms occur than are officially recorded by the arresting authorities. Nonreporting of criminal behavior occurs in many cases because the offense is known only to the one who commits it, or the victim is unwilling to report it. Thus, the number of recorded arrests of the inebriates must be presumed to underreport the violations which actually occurred. Furthermore, the particular charge on which an individual is booked may not represent the true violation, since offense charges are frequently altered according to the discretion of the functionaries of the legal system.

In spite of these limitations in the police recording system, an attempt was made to determine by statistical test whether any significant differences existed among the three subgroups in terms of their major social characteristics. The results were negative with respect to racial status, nationality background, religious affiliation, occupational status, and marital status. In terms of their previous criminal records the three subgroups evidenced slight differences which may have been due to chance, failing to attain a .05 level of confidence. Thus, the criminal records of the men in this sample do not serve to differentiate them into distinct behavioral subcategories which could be utilized for further analysis.

Notwithstanding these negative results, the interviews with the men revealed that the criminal record and type of activity in which the inebriate has engaged are used as means of evaluation and status placement by his colleagues. Since the system of clique differentiation and rating within the larger category of inebriates was not a major focus of the present investigation, only certain insights which relate to the status hierarchy can be offered, and they should not be viewed as conclusive until empirical studies are made. Among the men in the present sample, the individual with a record of convictions for felony offenses is not highly rated by the majority, who have only been in difficulty with the law as a result of their drinking pattern and were arrested only for public intoxication and related offenses. But certain types of offenders are viewed with more disfavor than others, and one of the least favored is the petty thief whose proclivities lead him not only to prey on society but on his fellow inmates. The petty thief may attempt to conceal his previous convictions on this charge, not only from officials and researchers but particularly from his fellow inmates, because of the negative values attached to his behavior. Negative evaluation is also made of the man who becomes abusive and engages in assaultive behavior under the influence of alcohol, since the aggression may be directed toward his peers as well as other members of society. This type of offender may have a history of arrests on the charge of aggravated assault. Unlike the situation in many long-term penal institutions, no positive status is granted the individual who has had an active criminal career with service in the "big leagues" of state and federal prisons. But perhaps the most disesteemed of all are those inebriates who are "panhandlers" and ply their trade even while incarcerated by attempting "to put the bite on" a fellow inmate.

The least disesteemed are those whose only encounter with legal authority has been for intoxication or closely related offenses, such as disorderly conduct and vagrancy. This is apparent in two ways: (a) the tendency on the part of some men to conceal their previous active criminal history, and (b) the graphic and emphatic assertion, by those who have only alcohol-related offenses on their record, that their problem is not with the law but with drinking.

From this detailed presentation of the previous criminal records of the chronic police case inebriates, certain generalizations may be abstracted:

(A) These men exhibit a high degree of heterogeneity in respect to their previous offenses in terms of types and frequency. The most common violation is public intoxication, with a mean of 12.8 arrests per man and a median of 6.0. But there is also a mean of 3.7 arrests per man, with a median of 3.0, on charges other than public intoxication. Moreover, the recorded number of arrests decidedly underrepresents the actual number of violations of the criminal code, many of which remain undetected, reflecting the vicissitudes of crime detection and reporting.

(B) An examination of the criminal histories of the chronic police case inebriates reveals that many have become what may be termed institutionalized offenders. This is reflected in their constant movement from the protective institutional environment of the penitentiary to the sheltered milieu of Skid Row or other forms of semi-communal living, such as work in hospitals or labor camps or residence in public shelters or cheap rooming-houses or hotels, and

return to the most protective environment of all—the penal institution. Thus their problem is not only one involving difficulties in
the sphere of drinking behavior but a much more deep-seated disorder referable to the psychological and social factors of dependency
and security.

The penal institution is thus functional for those inebriates who
show long and continuous histories of incarceration, in that it meets,
although in a socially disapproved way, the basic psychological
needs of their personality structure. Incarceration, on the other
hand, is dysfunctional in the sense that it provides the situation
in which the developing dependency can be fixed in the personality
pattern where it is already evident as an inability to develop au-
tonomy in adulthood.

Social Class Background

No student of human behavior can ignore the tremendous impact which socialization in a particular class pattern has upon the
personality development of the individual. A child is born into the
class position of his parents, and the process of learning the patterned ways of behaving that mark each class level occurs both in
overt and covert form. The class position will determine for each
individual the values, norms and standards which he uses to govern
his activities, will allow him a given degree of access to the rights,
privileges and obligations of the total society, and will establish the
criteria by which his goals are pursued. Each class level in society
may be viewed as possessing a unique subcultural way of life. This
may conflict in varying degrees with the cultural pattern of the
total society, or of other subcultural groups within the society.

Division into social classes occurs, however, on a community level,
and it is extremely doubtful that social class positions with identical
names, such as upper-middle class, are truly identical as between
the large urban center and the small rural community. It is for this
reason that social class assignment, which is viewed best in the
framework of a community situation, cannot be completely successful for a category of individuals who are drawn from such diverse
geographic areas, community types and nationality and racial backgrounds as the chronic police case inebriates. A further complication
is engendered by the fact that the members of the group range in age
from 19 to 79 years and are thus products of different time epochs
in reference to family background. Admittedly, there is no diffi-

culty in assigning social class position to these men if their present situation is used as the criterion, since the fact of their frequent incarceration is indicative of a lower class position or at least of being declassed from a higher position in society. But what of their social class origins? In view of the methodological difficulties previously discussed, no attempt will be made to assign to each inebriate a specific class position of origin, but this does not preclude an attempt to identify the general classes of society from which they are drawn.

Crucial leads concerning the social class origin of the inebriates can be derived from an investigation of the educational and occupational backgrounds of the parents. Occupation and educational attainment, along with source of income, dwelling area, and type of housing are frequently utilized indices of social class, as can be discerned from an examination of the Index of Status Characteristics used by the Warner school (63). Thus one means of discerning the social class origins of the sample is to compare the occupational distribution of their fathers with that of the incarcerated inebriates themselves. The occupational classification utilized for the inebriate is his primary occupational skill, regardless of whether he has been recently employed at it. And the comparison reveals that the overall occupational distribution of the inebriates is slightly below that of their fathers. For example, 4.3 per cent of the fathers and only 2.2 per cent of the inebriates were professional, technical or kindred workers by training; 17.1 per cent of the fathers and only 0.5 per cent of the inebriates were managers, officials and proprietors, including farm operators. This last statistic, however, is not placed in its proper perspective unless it is realized that the majority of fathers in this category were engaged in farming operations, and it is extremely difficult to gauge their class position without further information. The case data indicate that many were operators of small subsistence or marginal farms, who would be categorized as lower-class in any social class arrangement. Approximately equal proportions of fathers and sons were clerical and sales workers (2 per cent) and skilled workers (22 per cent). In the unskilled occupations were 42.4 per cent of the fathers and 67.6 per cent of the sons. This difference is probably exaggerated since the occupations of 11.9 per cent of the fathers were "unknown or other," compared to 4.9 per cent of the sons, and it is unlikely that if the father had been engaged in a skilled occupation the son would have been unaware of the fact. From the evidence of family occupational background, then, the inebriates seem to be drawn from the marginal or lower-class groups in society, though there are exceptions to this generalization.

Another index which has been utilized to place individuals in the social class hierarchy is educational attainment. Education is now one of the crucial means by which individuals may climb the social class ladder, since it provides access to many privileges and rewards in the society. A comparison of the educational attainment of their fathers with that of the incarcerated inebriates themselves (Table 17) reveals some interesting facts. The educational level of the inebriates is considerably higher than that of their parents. For example, 29 per cent of the fathers and 6 per cent of the sons had never attended school; 43 per cent of the fathers and 36 per cent of the sons received only some grade-school training; and only 4 per cent of the fathers compared to 32 per cent of the sons finished grade school or 8 years of formal education. Further, a significantly higher percentage of the inebriates compared to their fathers attended or completed college. And finally, since educational information was not obtained concerning 21 per cent of the fathers, their representation at the lower levels of educational attainment is perhaps too low. The higher educational achievement of the sons, however, is not unexpected in view of the passage of compulsory school attendance laws in more recent times, the placement of higher premiums on education, and the smaller number of immigrants among the sons. Nevertheless the educational attainment of both the incarcerated inebriates (Table 9) and their fathers is skewed in the direction of lack of education when compared to the society as a

TABLE 17.—*Distribution of the Sample and their Fathers, by Educational Attainment (in Per Cent)*

	Fathers	Present Sample
No schooling	28.9	5.7
Part grade school	43.3	36.1
Completed grade school	4.3	32.3
Part high school	0.5	13.4
Completed high school	1.1	7.1
Part college	0.5	3.1
Completed college	0.5	2.3
Undetermined	20.9	0.0
Totals	100.0	100.0

whole. The particularly low educational attainment of the fathers—
only 2.6 per cent attended or completed high school or college—is
indicative of origin in the lower classes of society and in groups
whose achievement is handicapped by lack of educational skills.

It must be concluded that the social class origin of the chronic
police case inebriates is from the bottom of the scale. Their fathers
were marked by a low order of occupational skills and by relatively
little formal education. On the other hand, there is a small subgroup, comprising between 5 and 10 per cent of the sample, who
had their origin in the higher social class groups in the society,
who are marked by an extreme downward spiral of social mobility,
and are in every sense of the term "declassed" individuals.

This small but particularly interesting group of "declassed" individuals is represented in the following case history.

Case 3. Jim Forrest's father owned the general store in a small village
in South Carolina. He was a good businessman and a good provider,
and was not bothered by the meagerness of his grade-school education.
Jim and his two brothers worked in the store in their spare time, and
it was expected that the boys would follow in their father's footsteps and
carry on the business.

Mrs. Forrest, on the other hand, was an educated woman with a college
degree. She had taught school before her marriage and again after the
children grew up. Jim's four sisters, like their mother, were all given a
college education. Although Jim took a college preparatory course in
high school, was an "average" student, and took an active part in student
activities, he, like his brothers, terminated his schooling on graduating
from high school and went to work in the family store.

Mrs. Forrest was a strict disciplinarian and the "head of the family,"
while Mr. Forrest was the provider. Jim felt closer to his mother than
to the rest of the family.

Jim married when he was 22 and stayed on at the store for 5 more
years. Then, tired of being tied to the counter and wanting some independence, he took a job as a traveling salesman. His wife and family did
not approve of this change. Jim was arrested seven times for public intoxication during this period. Finally, after 10 years of marriage and the
birth of two children, Jim and his wife separated. He now began to
drink more heavily.

After 5 years on the road as a salesman, Jim drifted into carnival work.
He worked with the gambling concessions because of the "big money"
but finally, after 10 years of it, left because his conscience bothered him
about his part in "fleecing suckers."

When he was 45 Jim discovered that he had tuberculosis. He went
home to recuperate and entered a sanitarium there. His father and one
brother, who had remained with the store, were kind to him. They wanted

Jim to stay with them, but when he was discharged with the tuberculosis arrested, Jim decided he would be in the way, and left.

He tried carnival life again but found that he was not physically fit for the heavy work. He now feels that the only work available to him requires too much physical stamina, and he works only occasionally and reluctantly as a dishwasher.

In the past year he has served three terms for public intoxication. He goes on 2- or 3-days binges by himself, preferring his own company to that of his Skid Row neighbors. He stays at the Glorious Hotel, reputedly the worst "flophouse" in the city.

SUMMARY

The focus of this chapter has been on a delineation of the major sociocultural characteristics of the chronic police case inebriate. This information was obtained from interviews with 187 men, a random sample of those serving sentences at the Monroe County Penitentiary for public intoxication. Where possible, an attempt has been made to compare the incarcerated inebriates with the general population in the sample area, which is Monroe County, New York, and with other groups who have been studied as problem drinkers. The two groups most frequently utilized for comparison were (a) Bacon's sample of men arrested for drunkenness in Connecticut during a short period of time in 1942, referred to as arrested inebriates; and (b) Straus and Bacon's sample of patients seen in alcoholism clinics throughout the country.

The chronic police case inebriates can be briefly described in terms of their major characteristics as follows:

1. *Age.* The mean and median ages of the incarcerated inebriates are higher than those of the general male population of Monroe County, of arrested inebriates, and of patients seen in alcoholism clinics. The present sample is one of the oldest problem drinking groups to be studied, in that 45 per cent are over 50 years of age.

2. *Racial Background.* This sample is marked by a high proportion of Negroes (18 per cent) in comparison to their representation in the general population of Monroe County (2 per cent). Negro and white offenders are marked by age differentials: Two-thirds of the Negroes are under 45 years of age, compared to 30 per cent of the whites. The Negroes are primarily from a rural or small-town Southern lower-class background.

3. *Nationality.* The most frequent nationality groupings are English and Irish. Irish individuals compose 35 per cent of the

sample, but there is an increasing number of Irish with advancing age, especially after 45. Italians, although represented in significant numbers in the general population, compose only 2 per cent of the sample.

4. *Community Background.* Thirteen per cent were born in Monroe County and another 25 per cent were born elsewhere in New York State. Only 9 per cent are foreign born, and this proportion declines with decreasing age. In terms of the most typical community in which socialization occurred, 24 per cent are rural, 29 per cent are from villages and small towns, 33 per cent from cities of 25,000 to 250,000 inhabitants, and 14 per cent are from urban centers of over 250,000 population. Negro offenders are more frequently of rural and small-town origin. The migration from rural areas is a source of cultural discontinuities for the inebriates.

5. *Marital Status.* While 59 per cent of the men in this sample had at one time married, compared to 47 per cent of Bacon's arrested inebriates and 44 per cent of the homeless men studied by Straus in New Haven, this proportion is far lower than the 80 per cent of clinic patients. The observed frequency of divorces and separations is far higher at all age levels than in the general population. Only 4 of the 187 men were "married and living with spouse" at the time of study, all under 45 years of age. From a comparison with general population data, the expected frequency of never-married status would be 13 per cent, whereas the observed frequency is 41 per cent; and the expected percentage of marriages terminating in divorce, widowhood or separation is 11, whereas the observed frequency was 96 per cent.

6. *Educational Attainment.* Seventy per cent of the sample did not go beyond grammar school, compared to 68 per cent of Bacon's arrested inebriates and 40 per cent of the general population. On the whole, the incarcerated inebriates are an educationally disadvantaged group.

7. *Occupational Status.* In comparison with the general population, the incarcerated inebriates possess a low order of primary occupational skills, 68 per cent being unskilled workers, mainly laborers, 22 per cent skilled workers, and 3 per cent professional and allied workers, compared to 13, 46 and 22 per cent, in the respective categories, in the general population.

8. *Religious Affiliation.* The sample consisted of 42 per cent Protestants, 40 per cent Catholics, and 18 per cent who professed

no affiliation. There were no Jews. Religion, except in the case of groups such as the Jews who exhibit a specific culture pattern, appears less important as an identifying trait than nationality or ethnic status.

9. *Residential Mobility.* The group exhibits moderate mobility in a geographic sense: 63 per cent have lived in the community of present residence for a period of 2 years, compared to 89 per cent of alcoholism clinic patients. However, the present sample is marked by high residential instability in terms of the numbers of places of residence and the type of residence reported at arrest. Only 5 per cent of the incarcerated inebriates were living in their own home or apartment, compared to 55 per cent of the clinic patients; and only 6 per cent were living in homes of friends or relatives, compared to 23 per cent of the clinic patients.

10. *Criminal History.* The incarcerated inebriates exhibited a wide variety of criminal histories. The mean number of recorded arrests for all causes is 16.5; the median is 10.2. For public intoxication only, the mean number of arrests is 12.8 and the median is 6.0. This median is approximately the same as Bacon (3) found for individuals arrested on charges of public intoxication in Connecticut. The mean number of arrests on charges other than public intoxication is 3.7, with a median of 2.0. The "average" chronic police case inebriate has thus experienced some 10 arrests on all charges, and the offender with 30, 40 or more arrests is atypical, though composing a sizable portion of the total. These men form the hard core of the institutionalized offenders.

The sample could be divided into three subgroups by previous criminal record: (a) 31 per cent who had been arrested only for public intoxication; (b) 32 per cent who had been arrested, in addition, on charges probably related to the excessive use of alcohol; and (c) 37 per cent who have been involved also in serious violations of the legal norms of the society. Men in the latter group showed a tendency to abandon the criminal career after the age of 35 or 40 with an intensified pattern of public intoxication thereafter.

11. *Social Class Background.* The chronic police case inebriates are drawn heavily from the lower social class groupings in the society, as is reflected in the educational attainment and occupational classification of their fathers. In a small subgroup, however, a pattern of downward social mobility is evidenced, and these are in reality "declassed" individuals.

Chapter 3

DRINKING PATTERNS AND EFFECTS

THE MAJOR FACTOR which gives unity to the category of chronic police case inebriates is their excessive involvement in the use of alcoholic beverages. Although many of the men would deny that they are "alcoholics" and this belief can be confirmed in some cases by an analysis of their histories, or might be verified by medical survey, there is no question that the men are problem drinkers. Their drinking behavior, whether of daily or spree pattern, has involved all of them in difficulty with the constituted sources of authority in the society. In the present chapter, the foci of discussion are the use of alcoholic beverages, the social–psychological context of that use, and the physical and psychological effects of the drinking behavior. In the psychological area, the concern is with the attitudes of these men toward their drinking problem in terms of attempts to seek help for its resolution.

USE OF ALCOHOL

Most of the men began drinking during their adolescence. Although it is expected that the inebriates will show some unique drinking behaviors, patterns of preference for and use of certain types of beverages—beer, wine, spirits and nonbeverage alcohol—may be expected to characterize different epochs in their life career. This assumption will be explored in terms of earliest drinking experiences and current drinking behavior. The question, however, whether excessive use of various types of beverages has different physiological and psychological consequences for the individual cannot be explored in the present context.

The type of alcoholic beverages preferred and most frequently used during the earliest drinking experiences of the men in the sample was beer; it was preferred by 44 per cent of the inebriates and most frequently used by 51 per cent. Although spirits, representing the strongest beverage in terms of alcohol content, was preferred by 38 per cent of the men, it was most frequently used by 27 per cent. The discrepancies between preference and use can best be explained in terms of the differential cost and accessibility of beverages to the adolescent in our society. Wine was characterized

TABLE 18.—*Type of Beverage Presently Preferred, by Age Categories*

	Under 45 Years		45 and Over	
	N	%	N	%
Beer	23	33.8	25	21.0
Wine	17	25.0*	51	42.9*
Spirits	27	39.7	42	35.3
Nonbeverage alcohol	1	1.5	1	0.5
Totals	*68*	*100.0*	*119*	*100.0*

* Chi squared = 5.2; P <.05.

by low preference and infrequent use; fewer than 2 per cent of the men preferred it, while 7 per cent most frequently imbibed it. A surprisingly high proportion (16 per cent) preferred and most frequently used nonbeverage alcohol. This is explained by the circumstance that the earliest drinking experience of many of these men occurred during the Prohibition era (1920–1933)—a period characterized by extreme ingenuity on the part of many individuals in obtaining alcohol in diverse forms, such as "bathtub gin." It should be noted also that the sample includes a number of Southern rural natives whose first drinking experiences centered around typical local "home brewed" beverages. On the whole it appears that in their early drinking experiences the men generally drank what they preferred.

Table 18 compares the two major age groupings of the sample, under 45 and 45 or older, in reference to their present preferences for certain types of beverage alcohol. As will be demonstrated below, preference does not necessarily coincide with most frequent use. The specific question being tested is whether there is a significant difference in preference for various types of beverage between the two age groups. A significant value of chi squared is found only in the case of wine, while beer, spirits and nonbeverage alcohol show only insignificant differences. The older age group shows a greater preference for wine than the younger.

During their earliest drinking experiences, the type of alcohol preferred was generally the type most frequently used by these men. Does this convergence still characterize their present drinking pattern? Again the only statistically significant difference between present preference and usage is found in the case of wine (Table 19): 36 per cent of the inebriates prefer wine, but 56 per cent use it most frequently. This difference is highly significant in more than a statistical sense. Wine, with alcohol content greater than beer

TABLE 19.—*Type of Beverage Presently Preferred and Most Frequently Used*

	Preference		Most Frequent Use	
	N	%	N	%
Beer	48	25.7	37	19.8
Wine	68	36.4*	104	55.6*
Spirits	69	36.9	45	24.0
Nonbeverage alcohol	2	1.0	1	0.6
Totals	*187*	*100.0*	*187*	*100.0*

* Chi squared = 13.19; P <.01.

but less than spirits, is the cheapest beverage per unit of ethyl alcohol. Its wide utilization by these inebriates, and perhaps the extent of its preference, can be explained in terms of "the punch it packs" per penny of price.[1] Cost, for almost all the inebriates, is a crucial factor in determining the type of alcohol they will consume.

Being a chronic inebriate also involves changes over the years in the drinking patterns of these men, as in their preferences and uses of beverages. One aspect of this development is discernible in a comparison between the type of beverage preferred during the earliest drinking experiences and currently (Table 20).

The most noticeable movement is toward an increasing preference for wine. In their early drinking experiences only 3 of the men (2 per cent) considered this beverage their first choice; now 68 men (36 per cent) list wine as their first choice. The difference is statistically highly significant (P <.01). The statement of one man perhaps gives the best explanation for this change: "I prefer wine

TABLE 20.—*Type of Beverage Preferred During Earliest Drinking Experiences and at Present*

	Early Preference		Present Preference	
	N	%	N	%
Beer	82	44.1*	48	25.7*
Wine	3	1.6†	68	36.4†
Spirits	71	38.2	69	36.9
Nonbeverage alcohol	30	16.1‡	2	1.0‡
Totals	*186*	*100.0*	*187*	*100.0*

* Chi squared = 13.93; P <.01.
† Chi squared = 70.82; P <.01.
‡ Chi squared = 25.14; P <.01.

[1] The wines bought by these men are of course the cheapest brands of the most heavily fortified types, containing usually 21 per cent alcohol.

to whisky or beer, even when I have the money, because you get more for less money, and it sneaks up on you." The attribution of this latter physiological effect to wine has resulted in the appellation of "Sneaky Pete" to some wines. There is a concurrent movement away from beer and nonbeverage alcohol as preferred choices, with statistically significant differences (P <.01) between early and present preferences. It may be stated that the learning of drinking behavior occurred around beer and nonbeverage alcohol (because of Prohibition), and that beer is discarded because of its low alcohol content and relative cost. Only two men reported preferring nonbeverage alcohol at present. It may be assumed that the study group does not use "smoke" or other varieties of nonbeverage alcohol unless the usual forms of beverage are not available. It is obvious, too, that the number preferring spirits remains constant from the earliest drinking experiences to the present.

Changes in the type of beverage most frequently used are examined in Table 21. The same general trends which were evidenced in preferences for types of beverage between early and late drinking experiences assert themselves here. Wine shows most significant change in frequency of use; 56 per cent of the sample use it now, compared to 7 per cent in their early drinking experiences (P <.01). This means that about half of these men are "winos" who steadily drink the cheapest fortified wines. The frequency of beer and nonbeverage alcohol use decreases significantly from early to present drinking experiences (P <.01), while the frequency of use of spirits remains constant.

In summary, the drinking pattern of the chronic police case inebriates, as exemplified by preference and most frequent use of various types of beverage, undergoes a significant change from early

TABLE 21.—*Type of Beverage Most Frequently Used During Early Drinking Experiences and at Present*

	Early Use		Present Use	
	N	%	N	%
Beer	94	50.5[*]	37	19.8[*]
Wine	13	7.0[†]	104	55.6[†]
Spirits	50	26.9	45	24.0
Nonbeverage alcohol	29	15.6[‡]	1	0.6[‡]
Totals	*186*	*100.0*	*187*	*100.0*

[*] Chi squared = 37.36; P <.01.
[†] Chi squared = 100.16; P <.01.
[‡] Chi squared = 26.57; P <.01.

TABLE 22.—*Type of Beverage Usually Ingested at Onset, Peak and End of Drinking Bout*

	Onset		Peak		End	
	N	%	N	%	N	%
Beer	48	25.6	37	19.9	40	21.6
Wine	77	41.2*	127	68.3*	134	72.0
Spirits	59	31.6†	17	9.1†	6	3.2
Nonbeverage alcohol	3	1.6	5	2.7	6	3.2
Totals	187	100.0	186	100.0	186	100.0

* Chi squared = 25.96; P <.01.
† Chi squared = 27.83; P <.01.

to present drinking experiences. There is a movement, progressive with age and decline in social and physical resources, from non-preference and nonuse of wine to its greater preference and use, owing to its ability to provide the desired physiological effect at the lowest cost. Concurrently, there is movement away from preference and use of beer and nonbeverage alcohol. The preference and use of spirits remains almost constant.

Further insight concerning the drinking patterns of the inebriates can be derived from an examination of their episodes of intoxication. The drinking bout may be divided into three phases:[2] the onset, the peak, and the end. The types of beverage used during each of these phases is shown in Table 22. A definite pattern associated with the phases of the drinking bout emerges. At the onset 41 per cent drink wine, 32 per cent spirits, and 26 per cent beer, while hardly 2 per cent utilize nonbeverage alcohol. The sharpest change occurs at the peak of the bout: wine replaces much of the spirits and some of the beer. The differences in the use of wine and spirits between the onset and peak phases of the bout are highly significant (P <.01). In moving from the peak to the end phase of the bout, there is a further decline in the proportion of spirits users (from 9 per cent to 3 per cent) and a slight further increase in wine users (from 68 to 72 per cent). But these differences are not statistically significant. The use of beer during the three phases fluctuates slightly, from a high of 26 per cent at the onset to 20 per cent at the peak. Only a few men reported drinking nonbeverage alcohol, and this must therefore be considered an atypical pattern. It must be remembered, however, that there are individual patterns which deviate markedly from the over-all group pattern shown in Table 22.

[2] As has been done by Parreiras, Lolli and Golder (39) and Terry, Lolli and Golder (58).

Related to the type of beverages ingested is the duration of the drinking bouts. Wide variation is discerned in this area. Our sample is composed partly of spree, binge or periodic drinkers whose pattern includes intervals of sobriety; and then, as if physiological, psychological or social tensions have built up to a bursting point, they explode into a lengthy drinking episode. There are also daily addictive drinkers who, when not incarcerated, must have some type of alcoholic beverage "to get them going," as they say. And there are cultural excessive drinkers, particularly the Negroes, whose drinking episodes characterize their weekend activities. But on the whole, the time of the drinking episodes involves over 2 days for the majority of the men: 27 per cent drink in bouts lasting 2 or 3 days; 23 per cent average 4 to 6 days; and 19 per cent a week or more. Among the older men the spree is more likely to be brief. This is reflected in the fact that 7 per cent report episodes of not more than half a day in duration and 24 per cent drink in bouts lasting usually from half a day to a day.

In contrast to the preceding statistical portrayal of the use of alcohol, the following case history offers a qualitative picture.

Case 4. Earl Finnigan is a 57-year-old man of Irish and Scotch-Irish descent. He is a chronic repeater at the county prison, at present confined to the prison hospital with tuberculosis.

Earl says he comes from an "old fashioned home," stable, congenial and comfortable. The family was Catholic but went to church rarely. Earl, the youngest of eight children, quit school with parental approval, after completing the eighth grade, so that he could go to work and be independent. This was the only goal Earl had as a boy, and he cannot recall any parental prodding toward goals of any sort. His first job lasted only 2 weeks and he seemed to have no inclinations toward something permanent. His occupational record is a blank until he was 22 years old.

He then worked for 2 years in a shoe factory. At 24 he married and got a job at an iron works. Earl's wife died in childbirth 3 years later. This loss was perceived by Earl as the loss of all that gave meaning to his pattern of existence. He left his job, joined the Army, and started drinking heavily. Earl blames all his subsequent drinking on the break-up of his family life.

Earl had been shy as a boy, and he remains a solitary and retiring individual—except when drunk. Then he becomes aggressive. During his 4-year stint in the Army he was court martialed because of a fight and received a discharge which was neither honorable nor dishonorable. In 1932 and 1933 he was arrested twice for robbery and for assault with intent to rob.

Earl has no technical skills but likes farm work and is proud of his record as a farmhand. He states that he can go back to any place where he has worked. He has been doing this since his discharge from the Army. He prefers to work alone and he works hard when he is sober. But alcohol has become his goal: he works until he accumulates enough to go on a long spree.

When the "hankering" takes him, he would "move heaven and earth" for a drink. When he drinks, he does not eat, and he sometimes will drink for a month without eating. He says that he drinks anything and everything—"smoke," canned heat, anything that will give him a kick. He prefers spirits, however, and usually starts out with this and ends up with wine. He drinks until he is arrested.

He accepts his "touch of TB" philosophically, stating without remorse that his way of life has finally caught up with him and that if he had not been blessed with a good constitution it would have happened sooner.

Earl thinks of himself as a confirmed alcoholic and never expects to be anything else. He says there is nothing in life he enjoys more than "a good drunk."

SOCIAL–PSYCHOLOGICAL CONTEXT OF DRINKING BEHAVIOR

Knowledge in the field of alcoholism provides the gross insight that the socialization experiences of the chronic police case inebriates have been either markedly deficient or traumatic. Some psychiatrists feel that the alcoholic is characterized by extreme dependency needs which find some gratification, though on a nonapproved level, in excessive drinking. It is not our function to submit psychiatric hypotheses to test but to seek further insight on the problem of dependency. Viewed in a social–psychological light, there are social situations and living experiences which meet the individual's dependency needs, and their presence or absence should be noted.

The adult life histories of many of the men in this sample have featured rather lengthy experiences with institutional living facilities. These experiences provide the social–psychological context within which drinking is a patterned activity that serves their basic dependency needs. Before discussing the function of institutional life for these men, data on their actual experience of it will be presented.

Only 20 per cent of the men have had no experience of institutional living; 10 per cent served in the Merchant Marine or Coast Guard and 9 per cent in the Civilian Conservation Corps; 24 per cent have worked as hospital attendants and 14 per cent at resorts or as life guards—jobs usually including room and board as wages.

Finally, 44 per cent have lived in public shelters (including missions).[3] Service with the military forces and the Merchant Marine generally occurs early in their life careers, while working as a hospital attendant or at a resort occurs later in the occupational pattern. When the man begins to live exclusively in shelter facilities, such as the "Sally" (Salvation Army) or a rescue mission operated with evangelical goals, he has reached the nadir phase of his career pattern. However, since many people who are not members of this problem group also have extensive histories of institutional life, it is germane to inquire into the length of this experience. This is, of course, predicated on the assumption that long periods of institutional living not only meet basic dependency needs of some inebriates but result in demonstrable changes in the personality. There is an extremely wide variation in the duration of adult institutional living by the men in our sample, ranging from less than a year in 20 per cent to 15 years or more in 6 per cent. If the sample is divided into two groups, using 3 years as a possibly significant length of exposure to the patterns of institutional living, then 48 per cent of the men have had this much exposure.

What, then, is the significance of this high incidence of contact with institutional patterns of living? There is no information available on the extent of institutional living for members of the general population, and among the younger generation—since 1940—most of them have been in the armed forces for 3 years or more. Institutional living of this extent alone cannot be assumed to have resulted in demonstrable changes in the personality which would be reflected in pathological drinking. We are no doubt dealing with a specially predisposed group in which institutional living functions to enhance the tendency to become dependent on drinking. Many of these men felt that their drinking pattern changed significantly while they were in the institutional setting; they believed that they began to drink with greater frequency and intensity. The validity of this belief is open to question but the body of knowledge concerning the culture patterns of these institutions lends some support to it.

The institutional setting, as typified by the military service or the Merchant Marine, represents an artificial environment when compared to the society as a whole. Generally this type of nonfamily male milieu places the minimum of demands and expectations on

---

[3] The percentages total more than 100 because many of the men have had more than one type of institutional living experience.

the individual aside from his specific assignments. There is no community of opinion or paramount social control over the behavior of the individual in the personal sphere. On the other hand, for the extremely dependent individual, the environment is well ordered in the sense that he is free from having to make anxiety-provoking decisions and his basic needs of shelter, clothing and food are generally provided. His intimacy needs can be met in the congregate environment on an undemanding level of interaction. But basic to all this is the organization of leisure time, as on weekends, particularly around a well-institutionalized pattern of drinking behavior which has the support of the norms of the institutional community. Without familial and other primary-group ties to provide for the meeting of basic social and psychological needs, and with an ordered but monotonous existence in an all-male environment, the individual moves into the cultural pattern of drinking which characterizes these institutions. He is further socialized to the value and necessity of the drinking behavior by the peers in the institution.

The Army, the Navy, the work camp, the railroad gang, and the lake steamer, all are rich in drinking culture. In these groups the harsh, the monotonous and the protective but controlled routines are broken by the nights, weekends and lay-offs which offer opportunities to drink. Drinking is a preoccupation and conversations at work are filled with talk of drink. The imagery and love of drinking are built up through these talks and stories. Fantasy around future drinking episodes serves the function of reducing the impact of heavy jobs in heat and cold, and of alleviating dull routines, sexual deprivation, and the loneliness of the all-male group. Drinking becomes a symbol of manliness and group integration.

Admittedly, certain forms of institutional living attract individuals who already have a serious drinking problem because it is within this social context that they can continue to drink heavily while earning enough to pay for it. Hospital attendants of certain types fall into this category.

Thus the institutional way of living is a social context which may be functional both in meeting the basic dependency needs of these men by its well-ordered routine and in providing a setting in which hard drinking is an accepted and even a rewarded pattern of behavior. It may be attractive both to those who are beginning to establish a heavy drinking pattern and those who already have a serious drinking problem.

The following case history briefly illustrates a career of institutional living:

Case 5. Mitch Michaels' parents had emigrated from Ireland and Scotland. They settled in Iowa, where Mitch was born; he was the oldest of three children, having one brother and one sister. Mr. Michaels was a farmer and Mitch helped with the chores. Mrs. Michaels was arthritic; she died when Mitch was 13. Mitch finished the 8th grade, then quit school to work on the farm with his father.

Mr. Michaels died when Mitch was 18, and Mitch then hired out as a farmhand, living in various farm homes. Although Mitch states that both his parents would have disapproved, he started drinking shortly after his father's death.

After 6 years as an itinerant farm laborer, Mitch joined the Navy, where he served 12 years. He remembers this as the happiest period of his life and wishes that he had stayed there. His drinking increased considerably in this environment.

Mitch was 35 when he left the Navy dishonorably discharged for bad conduct, and since then he has "floated around," working as a "gandy dancer" (railroad gang member) and at construction jobs. He thinks of himself as a "roamer" by nature, has no inclination toward marriage, and no serious attachments anywhere.

Mitch was first arrested for disorderly conduct while drunk when he was 40. He was jailed 8 times on this charge in New York City between 1938 and 1942. Altogether, he has been arrested 17 times for public intoxication or disorderly conduct. He is an aggressive person and appears to be in rugged health at the age of 55. He finds it more and more difficult to hold a job, since the job generally ends when he goes off on a drinking spree. The last 20 years were spent in construction and railroad work camps.

The drinking behavior of these men occurs in a social and socializing context. Drinking takes place in groups (Table 23). It is learned from associates in work groups and in drinking establishments which are the major and often exclusive places of recreation. These places are "the poor man's club" and the only institutions which welcome the transient, the unemployed, the unshaven, the not-so-clean, and the poorly dressed casual worker. The tavern, with its vested interest in the man's drinking, provides the only warmth and continual association available to him. This environment becomes a powerful influence for learning, maintaining and increasing drinking. Not only is it easy for the individual to drink

TABLE 23.—*Usual Types of Drinking Companions, by Marital Status (in Per Cent)*

	Single	Married, Separated	Divorced	Widowed; Married, Living with Spouse	All Marital Categories
None (drinks alone)	10.5	6.8	5.7	0	7.5
Other men	59.2	76.3	68.6	87.5	73.7
Women	0	1.7	0	0	0.5
Mixed, mostly men	15.8	11.9	14.3	12.5	14.0
Mixed, mostly women	2.6	3.4	11.4	0	4.3
*Totals**	*100.0*	*100.0*	*100.0*	*100.0*	*100.0*

* Percentages based on 186 cases.

but it is necessary for group integration, and he finds it affectively rewarding.

Table 23 presents an analysis of the men's usual drinking companions by marital status. Hardly 8 per cent are solitary drinkers— in sharp contrast with reports from certain Alcoholics Anonymous groups. The most usual companions are men: 74 per cent reported other men as their most frequent fellow drinkers and fewer than 1 per cent usually drink with women. Same-sex drinking groups provide the social context within which the inebriate meets psychological needs of intimacy, approval, recognition and security. The demands which the other members of the drinking group place upon him are limited, and he is able to handle these with his small competence in interpersonal relationships.

DRINKING GROUPS

Although the focus of this investigation was on the inebriates during their incarceration in the county penitentiary, observation of these men in their free milieu, Skid Row, revealed the existence of drinking cliques or groups. In many respects these groups are not different from those found in the larger society among noninebriates; at any rate, they are characterized by norms, expectancies and status differences among the members.

All the groups are exclusively male in their composition. This is in line with the overwhelming preference for other men as drinking companions. The groups are divided by age, however, mainly into two amorphous categories. One consists of men over 50 with old-age pension checks, no longer able to work, or in retirement. A favorite gathering place of this clique is Ma O'Conner's Cafe, where the hours are spent in passive verbal interaction with nostalgic overtones, in beer drinking and card playing. The other consists of younger men, generally under 50, who may be found in more active pursuits and places of recreation.

One of the younger groups, of almost exclusively Negro composition, has its gathering place at the Cosmopolitan Hotel Bar and Grill. The Negroes are mostly of southern rural or small-town lower-class origin who find some degree of unity in their similar cultural background and present situation. Their activities are of the more boisterous type, with an active verbal interchange among the members. Many peripheral clique members join the group for the Saturday night activities; some of these arrive in the urban center from the surrounding rural towns where much of the work week's leisure time had been spent in planning for the weekend of "recreation and relaxation" around the drinking activities. This is one of the few places in which the presence of women was noted.

Another younger group is described as the "bottle gang." Its membership is in many respects the best organized of such groups. Their activities are the despair of social workers, Alcoholics Anonymous members, policemen and clergymen who work for the rehabilitation of the inebriate. Among the welfare workers these men are known as the hard core who defy any attempt to adjust them to society. The bottle gang, generally "winos" who have served time in penal institutions for other criminal offenses, centers its interactions around drinking. There is a constant preoccupation with obtaining alcohol (in hard-pressed situations even nonbeverage alcohol is acceptable), ingesting alcohol, and—after release in the drinking bout—obtaining more alcohol to begin again.

The norms of the various groups do not include a high order of expectancies in the "middle class" sense. When the inebriate leaves the city he usually does so without being accompanied by another clique member. There are no set times for the meeting of the group, and rarely does any planned interaction, other than drinking, occur. Expectancies among group members generally center in three areas: (a) if one possesses either alcohol or money for alcohol, he will share his "good fortune" with other group members; (b) one will verbally interact with the other members, but respect for the privacy of the individual's past and family is maintained; and (c) mutual aid is provided in crises, e.g., sickness or threat of arrest.[4] The latter is an ever-present danger, as police "clean-up" campaigns come and go. The hostility toward the authority structure is reflected in the fact that some men refer to the police as "rag pickers."

The major function of these drinking groups, however, is in providing the context, social and psychological, for drinking behavior. In reality we have subcommunities of inebriates organized around one cardinal principle: drinking. The fantasies concerning the rewards of the drinking experiences are reinforced in the interaction of the members, who mutually support each other in obtaining alcohol and mutually share it. The group is perhaps the context in which the members alleviate each other's guilt and anxiety over the excessive drinking in which they indulge. But the sociopsychological functions of the drinking cliques as they exist on Skid Row need to be investigated more specifically.

TREATMENT FOR ALCOHOLISM

The help or treatment a group of men seek for their drinking problem represents in one sense their psychological attitude toward the problem. With the exception of occasional hospitalization enforced by the serious consequences of a spree, the individual must actively seek to be treated—otherwise he will get none.

What courses of action are open to the individual who perceives that he has a drinking problem and desires its amelioration? The Rochester community, at the time of this investigation, had two outpatient alcoholism clinics offering services at minimal financial charges, and a free alcoholism information center. These facilities, however, have no connection with the penal institution; the inebriate, therefore, must take the initiative in applying for help. Some judges do refer inebriates to the clinics, as an alternative to imprisonment, but generally they pick younger men with fewer arrests on their record. Hospital care for the extreme sequels of a drinking bout is available on Ward C3X at the County Hospital, but this provides only emergency treatment. The financial status of these men precludes treatment at a private sanitarium or rest home. The penitentiary serves as the rest home for these men, allowing them to rebuild their physical resources for the next spree. But

---

[4] These norms, observed in Rochester, N. Y., should be compared to those described by Jackson and Connor (25) from Seattle, Washington.

the penitentiary does not have treatment facilities for the drinking problem of the inmates. On another level, the fellowship of Alcoholics Anonymous offers hope for individuals who will adopt its program, and there is an active A.A. group in the penitentiary. But the initiative to attend A.A. meetings must come from the individual, and the program is successful only if the individual is adequately motivated. These are the types of treatment and resources available to the individual with a drinking problem but without money.

The actual experiences of the chronic police case inebriates with various treatment facilities are presented in Table 24.

The most revealing fact is that some 60 per cent of these men have never had any treatment for their drinking problem, and there is no statistically significant difference between those less and more than 45 years of age on this score. It is doubtful that the inpatient treatment obtained by 27 per cent of the inebriates mainly in the County Hospital ward was actually for their drinking problem rather than for the serious physiological consequences of a particular drinking bout. Only 11 per cent have been enrolled at outpatient clinics and these may be the only ones who have ever received any professional treatment for alcoholism.

Thus these inebriates as a group have obtained only the most cursory treatment for their drinking problem, and the indications are that they have not been motivated to seek such treatment. Further evidence of this is adduced below.

The last two decades have been marked by the widespread growth of Alcoholics Anonymous groups whose success in helping the problem drinker has captured the imagination of the public. Using the group as a therapeutic context, A.A. has brought sobriety to thousands who have been willing to accept the program enunciated in its famous "Twelve Steps" (1). The experience of the incarcer-

TABLE 24.—*Types of Treatment Experienced for Alcoholism, by Age Categories (in Per Cent)*

	Under 35	35–44	45–54	55 and Over	Total
Clinic (outpatient)	5.3	2.1	4.4	0	2.7
Clinic and hospital	0	6.4	11.7	8.0	8.2
Hospital (inpatient)	15.8	25.5	26.5	32.0	26.6
None	78.9	66.0	57.4	60.0	62.5
Totals	*100.0*	*100.0*	*100.0*	*100.0*	*100.0*

ated inebriates with A.A. reveals many significant facts. Almost half (46 per cent) have attended no meeting, although there are organized groups at the County Penitentiary, in the shelter facilities, and in the community at large. Only 12 per cent have visited meetings of regular A.A. groups in the community; 21 per cent have attended meetings in jails, 10 per cent in shelters, and another 10 per cent in both jails and shelters. Fewer than 2 per cent of those who had attended A.A. meetings held in jails and shelters have also gone to meetings of regular groups outside.

Besides information on actual experience with A.A., the attitudes of the men towards the fellowship were determined whenever possible. A few who had never attended claimed not to know what it was. But this was not typical. Most of the men chose to ignore the existence of A.A., regarding it as an organization for alcoholics —and although they have been arrested for drunkenness repeatedly they do not consider themselves alcoholics. In this sense, the name of the organization serves as a rationalization for avoidance and disinterest. Furthermore, some of the men have well-formed negative attitudes. One stated, in a very moralistic tone, "I don't care to attend A.A. and see someone trying to pick up another man's wife." The nonattender may also take the position epitomized by one respondent: "I never really tried it. I believe in it *but* not for myself."

Why do many of these men nevertheless attend A.A. meetings in jail? Although the manifest function of A.A. groups in the jail is for the alleviation of the individual's alcohol problem, they serve his more basic social and psychological needs. Some men frankly explained their attendance by three reasons: (*a*) to obtain free cigarettes, (*b*) to get out of the cell, and (*c*) to relieve the monotony of prison routine, with group associations as a byproduct. A.A. groups and meetings, as one of the few congregate activities approved by the penitentiary officials, allow the individual free movement and group associations which would be impossible otherwise. It is to these factors that attendance must be attributed, rather than the program or activities of the group directed toward the drinking problem.

As for the men who attended A.A. meetings only in the shelter facilities and missions which usually dot a Skid Row area, or in service centers for homeless men, this attendance is strongly recommended as a prerequisite to obtaining services from some of these facilities. It is much the same thing as "hitting the sawdust trail" (attending religious services) in order to receive shelter or food from some religious missions.

More favorable attitudes were expressed by the small percentage of men who had made contact with regular A.A. groups in the community. Among their comments were the following: "It's a club. It eases the mind to have someone who understands." "A.A. has the right approach. I received help from them in finding a job." "One finds friends there." But again, mere attendance at group meetings does not mean acceptance of the program. One man stated that he went to the meetings because he enjoyed listening to others narrate their experiences; while another goes only when he is hungry and destitute.

Each man in the sample was asked what effect he felt A.A. had had on his drinking pattern. It should be recalled that 46 per cent had never attended A.A. meetings. Of the remainder, approximately half (47 per cent) felt that the influence of attending such meetings on their drinking practices was negligible. Some of them claimed that A.A. activity only aggravated their problem and that they drank more after attending meetings. About one-third (36 per cent) felt that there was a slight improvement in their drinking pattern after contact with A.A. Some of these men felt better, but they stated that they "did not seem to get hold of the program." About one in six (17 per cent) felt that A.A. had brought about a definite improvement in their drinking problem. Since these men had been recently incarcerated for public intoxication, however, it is obvious that A.A. had not yet brought them the desired sobriety. Altogether, it is most obvious that these men are not psychologically ready for the A.A. program.[5]

In summary, the chronic police case inebriates have received little medical treatment and almost no psychological or psychiatric treatment for alcoholism. Hardly more than half of them have had some contact with A.A. groups, and these almost entirely in jail or in shelter facilities, but the effect of these contacts on their drinking problem has been negligible.

Physical Condition and Employability

The plan of this investigation called for a complete physical examination of each subject after a specified period for "drying out"

[5] The meaning and importance of "readiness" has been dealt with by Trice (59).

had occurred. A total of 148 medical examinations, including laboratory tests and chest X-rays, was obtained. The difference between the number of medical examinations and the number of men in the sample (187) is due chiefly to a change in medical personnel during the course of the investigation. In addition, several of the inebriates refused the medical examination after their social history was completed by the interviewer. Review of the social histories of the men not examined revealed no significant differences between them and the rest of the sample.

We were concerned particularly with the employability of these men, as an indication of the realistic possibility of their actual rehabilitation. Each man was therefore placed in one of four standard classes.

Class I. Men physically capable of performing most types of jobs.

Class II. Men physically capable of performing those duties with which they have a degree of familiarity or those types of employment which require moderate restrictions.

Class III. Men who are physically capable of performing only the lightest forms of work.

Class IV. Men 65 years of age or older, or who are physically unable to work and require domiciliary care.

Since the assignment of a man to a particular class was generally contingent upon the correction of an existent physical condition, a second classification was added:

0. No minor or major repairs needed.

1. Needs minor physical corrections or repairs, such as dentures, refraction, and the like.

2. Needs a major physical correction, such as repair of hernia.

3. Needs both major and minor physical corrections and repairs.

The distribution of the men according to this employment classification is presented in Table 25.

In considering the employability of these men, age is seen to be a crucial factor. Assuming that the necessary major and minor physical repairs have been made, hardly 6 per cent of those less than 45 years old are unemployable and require domiciliary care. Another 7 per cent are fit for only the lightest types of work. The remaining 87 per cent of these younger men are in classes I and II, indicating a high degree of employability.

The situation of the men aged 45 years or over is different. Approximately one-fourth (26 per cent) of them are not employable

TABLE 25.—*Employment Classifications, by Age Categories*

Classification	Under 45		45 and Over		All Ages	
	N	%	N	%	N	%
I (0)	3		0		3	
I (1)	16		5		21	
Total I	19	34.5	5	5.4	24	16.2
II (1)	27		34		61	
II (2)	1		2		3	
II (3)	1		3		4	
Total II						
III (1)	4		14		18	
III (2)	0		2		2	
III (3)	0		9		9	
Total III	4	7.3	25	26.9	29	19.6
Total IV	3	5.5	24	25.8	27	18.3
Grand total	55	100.0	93	100.0	148	100.0

even after physical repair; another 27 per cent are capable of performing only the lightest types of work. The largest proportion, 42 per cent, are capable of work which requires only moderate physical restrictions. Only 5 per cent of these older men are able to perform most types of work.

Taking the group as a whole, approximately one-fifth (18 per cent) are not employable. The remaining four-fifths are employable at tasks which may or may not require restrictions of a physical order. When these results are related to the employment records of these inebriates, as represented by the number of weeks worked in the year previous to incarceration and the number of jobs held,[6] an inescapable conclusion obtrudes itself. These men are not performing occupational tasks commensurate with their physical condition, assuming that needed physical repairs were made.

SUMMARY

In this chapter we have examined the drinking patterns of the chronic police case inebriates as discerned in the types of alcoholic beverages preferred and most frequently used both in early drinking experiences and contemporary drinking episodes. With the passage of time in their drinking careers these inebriates increasingly rely on wine for their bouts and less on beer or nonbeverage alcohol. The use of spirits remains relatively constant.

[6] These records are detailed in Chapter 6.

We have further examined the social–psychological context of the drinking episodes. The context of institutional living as experienced by these men represents a cultural configuration which is conducive to the learning and perpetuation of an excessive drinking pattern. Drinking occurs further in small intimate groups of men, which serve to meet the basic social and psychological needs of the inebriates in a social context suited to their limited skills in interpersonal relations. The expectations of behavior in the drinking groups are not as demanding on the individual as the marital or occupational expectations incurred in normal adult experience.

An index of psychological attitudes toward their drinking behavior was obtained by examining the steps taken by the incarcerated inebriates to obtain treatment for alcoholism. More than 60 per cent of the men had never received any treatment for their drinking problem in a hospital or clinic, and nearly half had never attended an Alcoholics Anonymous meeting. Of those who had attended A.A. meetings, nearly all had done so either while in jail or at a shelter, where the motivation for attendance was not related to the purpose of the fellowship.

Finally, the physical examinations of these men indicate that, if necessary minor and major physical corrections and repairs were made, nearly all of the men under 45 years of age are employable at some task, as are three-fourths of those 45 years of age or older.

Chapter 4

CHILDHOOD AND THE FAMILY

THE PURPOSE of the present chapter is to examine the up-bringing—the socialization experiences—of the chronic police case inebriates in their original families. Observers of human behavior are agreed on the pervasive role of the family in the development of the child's personality. Within the context of the family the child's fundamental needs for response, recognition, security, affection and approval are met. It is here that he learns the expectations of others and of society, and this prepares him to become a social being who lives in a social world. Furthermore, the family unit is the prime source of the values and standards of the society and of subcultural groups based on race, ethnic status, and economic differences.

The developmental history of these inebriates, from childhood to later maturity, are characterized by undersocialization both in the qualitative and quantitative sense. The term "undersocialization" is a broad one, encompassing much territory. In this study it means that an individual's life history is marked by a lack of participation in primary groups such as the family, play groups and peer groups, these being the sine qua non of personality formation. Participation in the core primary groups serves as the basis on which further social activities will be shaped. An individual who has had limited opportunities to develop intimate personal relationships in the primary groups is handicapped in sharing experiences with others; his interpersonal relationships are inept. But before discussing the family socialization experiences of our sample it is necessary to note some limits on the validity of the data.

The group under investigation is one of the oldest with a drinking problem to be studied; the median age is 47.7 years; 45 per cent are 50 years or older. Each subject was allowed by the interviewer to reconstruct his early history through open-ended questions and limited-response information questions. Two difficulties were encountered. First, the high median age of the respondents accentuated the factors of selective perception of long past events. In recounting old experience the individual tends to reorganize the perceptual field, and sharp peaks and curves will flatten with the passage of time. Significant episodes undergo an unconscious revision to bring them into harmony with the individual's "gestalt" of the past. For many, childhood and early family experiences are only vague recollections about an epoch with which they have not continued any active contact in their later years.

Another restriction on the data is found in the peer-group norms of the majority of these men, which limit the quality of the material the individual verbalizes concerning his original family. The tendency is to assign the responsibility for the present situation, if a problem is admitted, to factors other than those which occurred in the family of orientation, or to the unique personality configuration of the individual himself. This finds expression in the statement, "All the other members of my family are all right. I'm the black sheep." This statement in itself would make the observer skeptical concerning the family situation. In this sense, the group, while falling back on numerous rationalizations to explain their individual fates, do not exhibit any extraordinary aggressive tendencies toward parental models or society in general.

Structural Features of the Family

A primary concern in the investigation was to examine the structural aspects of the family of orientation, with the focus on its completeness as discerned by the presence or absence of the biological parents. The actual significance of the absence of one or both parents in an individual case is difficult to assess, but its probable crucial role in the child's personality development is widely accepted.

The records show that 23 per cent of the men lost their parents by death before the age of 15. In 16 per cent of the cases the family was broken by divorce or separation,[1] giving a total of 72 men, 39 per cent of the sample, whose families were broken before they reached 15 years of age.

This seems to be an extremely high percentage of families whose structure collapsed due to death, divorce or separation. Unfortunately, we do not possess exact comparable information concerning the general population, although data on other problem groups are available, particularly from studies of juvenile delinquency. In a

---

[1] This does not include families in which one or both parents died before the subject reached age 20.

study of 1,000 juvenile delinquents, by the Gluecks, 43 per cent came from homes broken early in childhood (20, *pp. 75–7*). Individuals who become involved in difficulty with the legal norms of society also appear to have come from broken homes more often than the general population (56, *pp. 142–4*).

What significance can be attached to the high rate of broken family structures among the incarcerated inebriates? It may be assumed that death, desertion and divorce do not represent the same order of effect on the individual, though they may create the same concrete problems in his developmental history. Divorce or desertion indicates that tension and discord have pervaded the emotional tone of the family and may have created unfavorable conditions for the personality development of the child. This is reflected in the following case history:

Case 6. Alfred Pond never knew his father, who deserted the mother shortly after the child's birth. He feels he was completely neglected as a child since his mother, a midwife, married twice after his father's disappearance and placed him with grandparents. The mother never took any interest in him and made no contribution to his growth or support. At 13 Alfred became dissatisfied with the conditions at his grandparents' home and ran away to live with an aunt, who hardly more than tolerated his presence during the next 6 years.

In this case the child felt unwanted by the father and mother who both rejected him by desertion; furthermore, he was placed in an emotionally sterile environment with grandparents whom he rejected. There is nothing in the family background to indicate that he ever obtained a satisfactory emotional linkage with any person, or had any stabilizing primary-group experiences.

Death, on the other hand, is a categoric risk at any time. It does not ordinarily carry social disapproval, and there are many institutionalized modes of adaptation to it. Its psychological impact on the personality of the child, therefore, may not be as far reaching as divorce or desertion.

Both death of a parent and divorce or desertion pose many questions in terms of the development of the child. On the practical level, the loss of the breadwinner may create insuperable problems in maintaining the family unit intact and may cause further structural disintegration. It should be noted that the family socialization period for the overwhelming majority of this group occurred before the enactment of protective legislation for the family unit under Social Security. On the most crucial plane of personality development, the loss of parents leaves a void in the existence of identification models which the child uses in shaping his role conceptions. The negative consequences of the lack of parental identification figures may be cancelled by the presence of other figures, but there is no guarantee this will be the case. In sum, the absence of one or both parents creates a condition in which the problems of socialization are multiplied, especially in the economic sphere and the realm of identification models, ego ideals and role conceptions. These are not insuperable problems in any child's socialization, but they are relevant in the case of the chronic police case inebriates, who were not favored by other conditions in the environment that would reduce the negative consequences of family disintegration.

In spite of this emphasis upon the structural features of the home, it should be realized that structural unity in no sense guarantees adequate socialization. The following case summary illustrates a family history marked by negative psychological features before the parents' separation:

Case 7. James Arthur's parents lived in Rochester, where he attended a parochial school. He recalls that his home was marked by the continual "bickering" of his parents, which resulted in his father beating his mother. James feels that the unhappy home situation was responsible for his running away at the early age of 14. He went to Chicago where he earned his living by working in restaurants and doing odd jobs. His parents made no effort to get him to return home and were divorced when James was 17. On his return to Rochester at 19, James found his father, who had always been a very heavy drinker, continuing on this course at an accelerated pace. His mother, who had been mentally ill, died shortly after his return.

GEOGRAPHIC MOBILITY OF THE FAMILY

Unlike the inebriates themselves, their families were characterized by rather stable residential location during the childhood of the subjects. Thus 73 per cent of the men reported that they had lived in only one community up to the age of 16 years, 19 per cent in two communities, and only 8 per cent in three or more communities. Information was not obtained, however, concerning the movement of the family within the community of origin, so that a higher degree of residential stability may be attributed to the families than actually is the case. On the other hand, these statistics suggest that the present mobility of the sample is not necessarily related to a pattern learned in the original family.

Participation in Religious Activities

Although the families of our sample appear to be marked by residential stability, they were not characterized by any high degree of participation in the activities of the community. This is not an unexpected conclusion, since they are drawn primarily from the lower socioeconomic group who are not frequent participants in formal organizations in the community.

It was felt that perhaps less bias would result if the index of community integration, at least in a minimal sense, were the degree and extent of participation in the religious institution, since this activity pervades all class levels in the society and shows adaptation to the lower levels of society in sectarian and evangelistic groups. In 34 per cent of the cases the men reported that their families did not participate in any religious activities, and in 23 per cent the participation was rare or infrequent. In 41 per cent family attendance at church was regular, but in only 2 per cent of the cases was this attendance combined with any other type of participation, as in guilds, men's clubs and choirs. Thus the inebriates in their original families were not exposed to any extent to the sharing of the extrafamilial community activities which are potential sources for the creation of close interpersonal bonds. As a group, they are marked by lack of experience in all types of sharing activities on the formal level of societal organization.

Adaptation and Integration of the Family

From the attitudes and opinions expressed by the inebriates in reference to their families of orientation, an attempt was made to determine the level of adaptation and integration of these families by a partial use of the Cavan scale.[2] This attempt was only partially successful in that the scale is biased toward the middle-class family and a fairly significant attrition of cases occurred in its application—10 to 25 per cent for various items—due to the incompleteness of data and the meaninglessness of certain scale items for the respondents and their family situations. Further loss occurs when the family unit was broken early in the history of the child. Despite the attrition rate, it is believed that the scale pattern provides an opportunity to consider generally the major features of

[2] The Scale of Family Integration and Adaptability by Ruth Shoule Cavan, reproduced completely in Burgess and Locke (9, *pp. 781–4*).

the integration and adaptation of the family units of our sample. But the data should not be viewed as final or conclusive.

The first item for analysis from the Cavan scale relates to the nature of the affectional bonds which the respondents perceived in their parents. Of 145 men, 26 per cent rated their parents as "estranged or detached," 14 per cent as exhibiting "minor disagreements" or "impersonal," 50 per cent as "average" or with "congenial love," and 10 per cent as "in love more than average." Not one thought his parents exhibited "intense romantic attachment." Obviously these perceptions may not represent reality as the parents experienced it. Nevertheless, the perceived quality of the parental relationship is influential in the development of the individual's affective qualities and contributes in subtle ways to the adult conception of the marital bond. And 40 per cent of these men perceived a parental relationship marked by detachment and negative emotional tone or quality, though the mode is one of "average" or congenial love.

Another index of the degree of integration of a family unit is provided in the relationships which exist among the children who compose it. The responses of 129 men on this item indicate that these relationships were not marked by any deep psychological ties: only 3 per cent felt strong or above-average affection for their siblings while 70 per cent reported "passing noncontinuous friction," 17 per cent "minor but continuous friction" and 10 per cent "serious friction" with their siblings. A considerable degree of emotional impoverishment in their immediate social environment is implied in the lack of any deep attachments to siblings, and this seems significant in the context of the socialization milieu of these men, which was primarily a folk-oriented class stratum with emphasis upon kinship. The family group of children did not form a spontaneous intimate primary group which would provide a basis for further group ties in adulthood. An ability to relate to siblings may be a prerequisite developmental phenomenon for the ability to relate to other people outside the context of the family unit.

The integration of a family unit can also be viewed in terms of the cooperation engendered among its members, not only in their routine daily duties but under the impact of sudden drastic changes in the environment or shifts in interpersonal relationships which are viewed as crisis situations. The families of the inebriates were marked by a high degree of unwillingness and reluctance in this sphere. In 35 per cent of the 139 reported family units there was "refusal to cooperate and absence of family goals," and in 21 per cent a "reluctance to cooperate and few family goals." In only 21 per cent were definite sacrifices made for the family in a crisis, and in the remainder moderate sacrifices not incompatible with the interests of the individual were reported. The significant finding is the almost complete absence of family units with well-defined family goals, with an emphasis on sacrifices to achieve goals through cooperative family endeavors. This picture does not accurately reflect the total situation, since families broken early in the subject's life have been excluded and these would exemplify a greater emotional poverty. The lack of a cooperative self-sacrificing philosophy in the family unit has implications for the future behavior of the individual. Essential experiences in relating to others, in sacrificing one's immediate needs and wants for future goals, and in family sharing associations upon which adult cooperative and sharing activities are built, were not obtained in the socialization process of these inebriates.

Still another way in which the integration and psychological unity of the family may be gauged is by the effect of tension in the family on the interpersonal relationships within it. The data show that in 28 per cent of the families ordinary tensions created major strains in the interpersonal relationships, in 15 per cent minor but lasting strains, and in 47 per cent some strain which, however, was not lasting. Only in 9 per cent of the cases was the unity or integration of the families sufficient so that tensions which occur with regularity in a family evoked only insignificant effects.

In summary, the families of the chronic police case inebriates were characterized by traits indicative of a low order of unity. This is seen in the perception of weak affectional ties between parents, in the indifferent relationships among siblings, in the lack of mutual cooperation or goals in the family, and in the disruptive effect of ordinary tensions on interpersonal relationships.

Families may be characterized further in terms of their adaptability to new situations and the degree of traditionalism and rigidity determining their behavior. The degree of traditionalism in reference to the mores can be discerned from the family leadership structure or the dominance pattern. Since this is a preponderately lower-class group, the results are not entirely unexpected. Among 146 reporting cases, paternal dominance prevailed in 53 per cent, maternal dominance in 33 per cent, and substantial absence of parental leadership in 11 per cent. The most significant item is the relative absence of the family in which both parents are equals (reported in 3 per cent), and the total absence of the family council type in which all members participate in the decision-making process.

One of the best indexes of the adaptability of a family is its capacity to make adjustments to crises, whether internally or externally engendered, when the patterned solutions created over time to meet the tasks of interaction in the family unit are no longer adequate to cope with a new position caused, e.g., by extreme financial pressure, serious illness or death, and a new pattern of behavior and adaptation by the family members must be found. The negative effects of crises in the families of the incarcerated inebriates is shown by the fact that among 140 reporting cases poor or problematic adjustments were made in over three-fourths. Only in 6 per cent was a crisis met with a satisfactory adjustment, while in 18 per cent no crisis situation was discerned. The inability of the family unit to resolve crises has its impact in the young member's lack of experience and resources in handling such situations as they occur in his adulthood and in psychological attitudes which hinder flexible movement from conventionalized ways of behaving to meet the new exigencies. In short, these families are marked by a concentration on the negative side of a continuum, when viewed in terms of integration and adaptation.

MOTHER–SON RELATIONSHIPS

In assessing mother–son relationships, reliance has been placed upon the verbalized responses of the men during the interview. This approach suffers from the limitation that the verbalized attitude may not truly reflect the deep-seated emotions which govern the behavior. Projective personality devices would have accomplished this task with greater reliability. Nevertheless the responses of an individual concerning this crucial relationship cannot help reflecting some of its inherent quality.

The verbalized attitudes of the inebriates toward their mothers may be described as stereotyped positive orientation in 55 per cent of the cases, and highly positive feeling in 5 per cent. Significantly, 23 per cent expressed negative or highly negative sentiments while 16 per cent gave essentially neutral responses, neither positive nor negative. These percentages are based on 130 cases. The impression was gained that the positive orientation to the mother represents in considerable part the operation of stereotyped responses dictated by the culture: our society strongly taboos any free verbalization of antagonism toward the mother figure, which is never a proper object of aggressive behavior. In this light the negative expressions of nearly one-fourth of the men are remarkable. On the other hand, there are indications that the dependency pattern found in the inebriates' reliance on institutional facilities in later life may be related to the formation of an overdependent relationship to the mother. Further evidence of the sensitive nature of this basic relationship is discerned in the high attrition of responses in questions relating to the mother, suggesting that many of these men had not achieved a satisfactory resolution of this fundamental relationship.

Despite the existence of the dependency syndrome, there are many indications of frequent rejection of the child by the mother. When questioned further on whether they felt they had been "brushed off" or ignored by their mothers, 23 per cent of the men gave an affirmative answer and 26 per cent were uncertain. Only 51 per cent definitely denied rejection by the mother.

The men were also asked to characterize their mothers' behavior toward them. The dynamics of the mother–son relationship are best revealed in these responses. The most frequent characterization (58 per cent) portrayed a mother with a flat tone of affect, as evidenced in her neutrality toward or disinterest in the activities of the son. Gloomy or depressed is the picture in 13 per cent of the cases, and strict, cruel or harsh in 12 per cent. Only 17 per cent of the men remembered a mother who was understanding and kind, with positive qualities of affect. The tone of the primary group set by the mothers is one of psychological impoverishment in terms of affective qualities, and these inebriates in their early life experiences were deprived of the warm spontaneous expressions of emotion and feeling that are essential in the socialization experience. It is difficult not to suspect that the majority who expressed positive feelings toward the mother figure were making culturally stereotyped responses and that their relationship with the mother was marked by emotional deprivation.

An indirect way of viewing the mother–son relationship is in terms of the mother's active role in teaching the child how to do particular things, or working with him to develop his supplemental skills for activities in general. Only 14 per cent of the men felt that their mothers had taught them such things as domestic tasks, hobbies, recreational skills, or provided them with the facilities and amenities of social behavior.

In summary, although the chronic police case inebriates show a strong tendency to verbalize positive attitudes and feelings toward their mothers, many negative subtleties of the relationship are hidden behind this facade. The mother is often a figure without affect, and disinterested in the child's activities. The dependency relationship which the child sought to create is set in perceptual distortion and is not reciprocated by the mother, but the problem is still unresolved in a socially accepted way by the adult man. In many cases the pattern involves rejection by the mother, which is perceived and reacted to by the son. The general thread that runs through the cases is an emotionally impoverished relationship between mother and son, with consequent deprivation of social and psychological gratifications which are usually found in the primary group of the family.

Father–Son Relationships

The procedure for studying the mother–son relationship was used also for the father–son relationship, and the same limitations apply.

The verbalized attitudes of the men (125 cases) again show the stereotyped favorable response pattern, though not to the same degree as in case of the mothers. Not one man was highly positively oriented toward his father, though just over half, 51 per cent, expressed positive sentiments. Approximately one-third (34 per cent) showed a highly negative or negative attitude toward their fathers, while 14 per cent exhibited disinterest or neutrality. Expressions of neutrality are probably negative feelings covered by a cultural veneer.

Each subject was asked to characterize his father's behavior toward him. The characterizations of the fathers are even more negative than were those of the mothers. "Cruel, strict or harsh" was applied to 24 per cent of the fathers, compared to 12 per cent of the mothers. The most frequent characterization (56 per cent) was neutrality, disinterest and lack of affective quality in the relationship. "Gloomy and depressed" was attributed to 12 per cent; "kind and understanding" to only 8 per cent. That over 90 per cent of the fathers were characterized negatively, coupled with the depiction of the mothers, strongly indicates an emotional environment characterized by social and psychological deprivation. The important fact is that the warm, supportive relationships essential for the development of primary task skills were not nurtured by the psychological attributes of the fathers of these inebriates.

The slightly more negative tone of the father–son relationship can be discerned further from the men's answers to the question whether they had been "brushed off" by their fathers. Fully 36 per cent felt they had been neglected or ignored, while 42 per cent did not feel so and 22 per cent were uncertain. The widespread feeling of having been rejected by parents is unmistakable.

The father as the primary male figure in the individual's immediate social environment serves as the identification model in the son's socialization, the one from whom the child unconsciously learns the expected or appropriate male roles. As has been noted, the families of the inebriates were characterized by a high rate of broken homes. Mere physical presence of a male figure in the environment may not be sufficient to ensure identification with the male social roles, which is built upon a reciprocal interweaving of the personalities of the man and the boy during the course of multiple intimate associations. The poverty of the inebriates' relationship with their fathers is revealed in their responses to the question of sharing in activities such as sports, fishing, hunting, hobbies, or other personal or leisure-time activities. In 83 per cent of the cases there was no such sharing.

Another index of father–son interaction is the extent to which the father teaches his son how to do such things as are involved in sports, household chores, and social life. Two-thirds of the inebriates felt that they had not had this sort of relationship with their fathers.

Though not spelled out in fine social and psychological detail, gross conclusions may be drawn from the quality of the father–son relationship as pictured in the verbalized responses of the inebriates. The scant social interaction between fathers and sons, the sons' perceived rejections by their fathers, the limited emotional support, both in depth and tone, provided by the fathers, and their failure as identification models for building social roles, all add up to the fact that the crucial relationship of father and son was marked by sheer inadequacy. The core of undersocialization finds its first expression in the lack of sustaining primary-group relationships with either the father or the mother in the early environment of the chronic police case inebriates. From this stems their inability in later developmental epochs to build the sustaining primary-group relationships through which individuals can alleviate the anxieties that derive from secondary roles, including those related to marriage and occupation.

The following case history illustrates the father–son relationship demonstrated above.

Case 8. Because Harvey Seymeyer's life represents basically a series of responses to one person, his father, it is necessary to give the stories of both father and son almost equal emphasis. Harvey is now 51. The father figures as importantly in his life now as when Harvey was a child.

Harvey's father is a "tight-fisted, bull-headed," methodical German, now living on a pension from the firm that employed him for 30 years. Mr. Seymeyer has always lived a neat and orderly life and sees no reason why Harvey, his only son, should not do the same. Mr. Seymeyer paid no attention to Harvey except for disciplining the boy, and showed no sympathy or generosity toward his "weaknesses."

Harvey had a more rewarding relationship with his mother, an Irish Catholic with a more sociable and sympathetic nature. Mr. Seymeyer, however, considered his wife much too "soft," and he was the head of the house. Consequently, although Mr. Seymeyer tried to instill his own values into his son, Harvey grew up with one all-prevading ideal—to get out and away from his father. This goal, however, which the son has never yet quite fulfilled, is complicated by the apparent fact that Harvey has never given up his dependency on his father.

Harvey is small in stature and has always felt handicapped by this. To illustrate this point, Harvey often tells of how when he was 18 and all his friends were enlisting in the Navy, he, because of his small size and immaturity, was sent home to get parental approval. His father refused. Harvey got drunk for the first time at the going-away party for his gang.

In spite of his size, Harvey excelled in sports but his father never exhibited any interest in this and cared only about his work record. To compensate for his handicap, Harvey developed a "cocky" and aggressive manner. He quit school after the 9th grade in order to go to work and earn his own money, and got a job as an errand boy but had to bring his earnings home. He was, however, given a larger allowance and found that he enjoyed being free to roam the town and do as he pleased.

Subsequently, Harvey worked for 10 years in a shoe factory, 4 years for a stove company, and 2 years for a radio manufacturer, all in his home town. He finally got into the military service during the Second World War. His army career lasted 3 months, and part of it was spent in the stockade for insubordination.

At the age of 36 Harvey married. His drinking had increased in the

Army and it now reached a magnitude that became a major factor in the break-up of his marriage 3 years later. He has had no contact with his wife and child for 12 years.

Harvey became a "habitual" drinker after the break-up of his marriage and the death of his mother, which occurred in the same year. He cannot keep up with the alcohol intake of his cronies, however, and after 2 or 3 days on a spree he becomes helpless and is arrested. Before Harvey's mother died she had made her husband promise to help their wayward son. Harvey states that his father never cared about him until his mother died, and now he resents his "meddling." He will accept his father's help only when he is down and out.

Mr. Seymeyer hates to think of his only son and heir as an alcoholic. He will ignore Harvey on the street for fear that someone will realize that he is the father of this "drunken bum." Every time Harvey is released from the county prison, however, Mr. Seymeyer helps find him a job and obtain a room. He is candid in saying that he would like to find some place where Harvey could be put away permanently so that he would not have to worry about him.

Harvey has been arrested 15 times in the last 4 years for public intoxication. He makes a good prisoner. He works well and is cooperative, and his associates like having him around. But as soon as he is released he "hits the bottle." He is "awfully tired" of hearing from "old friends" that the least he can do is straighten himself out for the sake of his father.

The Family as a Primary Group

The foremost socializing agency is the family, and it is one of the basic primary groups of society along with certain types of peer groups and friendship groups. The most adequate conceptualization of the primary group and its implications for personality development is that of the late Charles Horton Cooley. He wrote (10, *p. 23*):

By primary groups, I mean those characterized by intimate face to face association and cooperation. They are primary in several senses, but chiefly in that they are fundamental in forming the social nature and ideals of the individual. The result of intimate association, psychologically, is a certain fusion of individualities in a common whole, so that one's very self, for many purposes at least, is the common life and purpose of the group . . . . The most important spheres of this intimate association and cooperation—though by no means the only ones—are the family, the play group of children, and the neighborhood or community group of elders. Primary groups are primary in the sense that they give the individual his earliest and completest experience of social unity, and also in the sense that they do not change in the same degree as more elaborate relations, but are a comparatively permanent source out of which the latter are ever springing.

That for the chronic police case inebriates the primary-group socialization experience was deficient, resulting in a pattern of undersocialization, has been shown by a number of measures, including a high proportion of structurally broken families, poor adaptation and integration of the family unit, and inadequate relationships with many of the mothers and even more of the fathers. Certain additional techniques can be employed to test the functional quality of the inebriates' families as primary groups.

Primary groups, according to Kingsley Davis (15, *pp. 289–294*), flourish best when certain prerequisities are fulfilled: smallness, duration, and intensity of association. Family groups are always small in size and generally are marked by long duration in relation to other groups; thus these factors in the equation present no difficulty. Intensity is a variable in the formula and will show differences. It is built by frequency. For individuals to develop interpersonal ties they must be in frequent interaction, preferably face to face. If they do not interact frequently, the vines of personal ties atrophy. An attempt to determine the kind of interaction usual in the families of the inebriates yielded the following results:

In 150 cases, interaction between family members, limited chiefly to mealtime activities, was the rule in 35 per cent. Interaction limited to necessities and occasional leisure-time pursuits was the rule in another 56 per cent. Only in 9 per cent of these families was there interaction of a quality that could be termed intensive or conducive to the formation of substantial primary-group ties. A decisive precondition for the formation of primary groups is not met in the examination of these interaction frequencies.

As Cooley (10) pointed out, the primary group creates the conditions that allow for a blending of the personalities of the group into a whole, so that the self becomes "the common life and purpose of the group." If that be the case, this result should find expression in a general satisfaction on the part of the individual with the existent conditions of the group's activities. The individual is immersed in the activities and common life of the group and finds them gratifying. In the hope of testing the satisfaction level in the family groups of the present sample, an extremely simple question was posed: "Was home a good place to be?" Fewer than half—47 per cent—replied that in general home was a good place to be, but 23 per cent felt that no categorical answer could be given, and 30 per cent gave negative responses, feeling that there were no signifi-

cant positive features in the home situation. As far as these verbalized responses are concerned, there was no decided sense of satisfaction with the home situation in a majority of the cases.

The most important feature of the family as a primary group is
in providing the individual with his first sense of social unity and
belongingness to a structure of other persons outside himself. In
achieving the sense of belongingness, the individual no longer perceives himself as an isolated atom but is able to use the security
that results from attachment to a structure larger and outside himself to develop other personal relationships. The lay analyst, Erik
Erikson, has established the proposition that the incorporation of
trust of significant others in opposition to basic mistrust of others
is the primary block on which further socialization proceeds (16).
The creation of trust as a fundamental attribute of the personality
is built around the sense of belongingness and security which the
child obtains from the primary group of the family. An attempt
was made to discern to what extent the families of the inebriates
developed this attribute by recording the subjective feelings of the
men in reference to the sense of belongingness to their family units.
This was done by constructing a continuum of four points arranged
horizontally in the following order: (a) well integrated; (b) integrated with some negative features; (c) negative feelings pre-
dominate, with some integration; (d) rejection. The distribution
of cases occurred in the following proportions: 19 per cent felt
well integrated with their family groups; 33 per cent felt only a
token sense of belongingness marked by the predominance of
negative feelings concerning their acceptance; and 20 per cent had
no sense of belonging to the family group and classified themselves
as rejected children. Thus only about one in five expressed the ideal
sentiments of belongingness that characterize primary-group relationships.

The following brief case summary illustrates the complete absence of the primary group or the feeling of belongingness:

Case 9. Richard Bailey, now 59, represents an inveterate type of
chronic police case inebriate. He never knew his father and is not sure
whether his mother was legally married, since the father deserted when
he was an extremely small child. His mother has been married three
times; at least, she has lived with three different men. She gave little
attention to Richard, reserving her interest for her men friends. As he
phrases it, he "grew up like Topsy," without anyone paying attention
to him. His early life was marked by frequent moves from one blighted

area of the city to another and by working after school to help support himself. At 16 he went to work on Skid Row in a restaurant and began to live in the "flops" above the saloons.

Bailey's life history, beginning with the rejection by the parents and the lack of any adequate substitute figures to provide him with social integration and psychological gratification, is characterized by existence on the most marginal level.

In this section the undersocialization of the incarcerated inebriates has been revealed by the deficiencies in their family primary groups, by the infrequency of interaction among family members, by the inebriates' feelings of dissatisfaction with their original home situations, and by the absence of a sense of belongingness in relation to their families.

SUMMARY

The primary focus of this chapter has been on the early socialization experiences of the chronic police case inebriates in their original families. Despite certain inadequacies of the data, the general hypothesis of undersocialization due to deficiencies in the family setting remains plausible and should be investigated further and in greater depth.

The general proposition of inadequate socialization is supported by the following data:

1. The structural continuity of the family units was broken by death, divorce or separation before the inebriates' fifteenth birthday in 39 per cent of the cases.

2. The families largely failed to participate in community activities.

3. Application of a modified Cavan scale showed the level of family integration and adaptability to be low.

4. Mother–son and father–son relationships, even as distorted by culturally stereotyped responses, evidenced a trend in the direction of serious deprivations for the inebriates in meeting their basic emotional, social and psychological needs.

5. The sense of belongingness achieved by membership and acceptance in a social unit larger than the individual himself, such as the family primary group, was only partially achieved by most of the inebriates.

Chapter 5

ADOLESCENCE

THE ADOLESCENT socialization experiences of the chronic police case inebriate is the topic of the present chapter. Adolescence is viewed here as covering a broader chronological period than just the few years after physiological puberty; it lasts from the child's first ability to enter into meaningful relationships with same-sex peers to his establishment of some sense of social and psychological identity. This scheme carries us from the stage in development which is called preadolescence by Harry Stack Sullivan[1] to the fifth stage of man as considered by Erik Erikson (16). The frame of reference for viewing the adolescent phase of development will be largely in terms of assumptions concerning the development of personality made particularly by Sullivan as well as those of Erikson and Allison Davis (12).

The previous chapter presented evidence that the childhood socialization experiences of the inebriates in their families were inadequate, and that as a group they were marked by undersocialization and serious deprivation of basic social, emotional and psychological needs by their parental figures. But our assumption is that personality is developmental and dynamic, and that although unfortunate experiences on one level of development may handicap the individual in the learning and performance of biological, psychological and social tasks at a later stage, an "infantile determinist" position in reference to personality is not acceptable. Personality can be molded and does change after childhood. One of the positive functions of entrance into school and participation with other people, under favorable conditions, is the alleviation and repair of childhood traumas. Furthermore, personalities characterized by a negative direction or orientation can be recast in more positive directions by the types and qualities of their experiences at a later period, after childhood (51, *p. 227*). The crucial point is that unfortunate experiences of early socialization, such as emotional de-

---

[1] The particularly stimulating influence of Harry Stack Sullivan on the conceptualization of this chapter cannot be overestimated and the authors are highly indebted to Sullivan's writings for many of his generalizations. For example see his *The Interpersonal Theory of Psychiatry* (51).

privation and deficiency, may become reshaped and of little significance when socialization experiences with the childhood and peer groups are sufficiently positive. Thus it is necessary to examine the nature of the adolescent socialization experiences of our sample and to determine the general trends of their effects.

Analysis of adolescent socialization experiences is essential in terms of the frame of reference we are using for personality formation, i.e., one of the stages of development of personality. Developmental stages, in one sense, are ideal constructs, for as conceptualized by both psychiatrists and sociologists, stages blend and fuse into one another and do not cease with the onset of puberty, as implied in Freud, or with adulthood where Sullivan ends his discussion. Developmental stages are continuous throughout the life cycle as is noted by Erikson (16, *pp. 219–234*) in his eight stages of man and by Havighurst (23) in his presentation of the developmental tasks that are associated with chronological periods in the life cycle of the individual. All of these writings emphasize that certain biological, psychological and sociocultural needs are of primary importance at certain chronological periods in the life cycle. The cultural context in which socialization occurs, however, will cause variations in the primacy of needs at particular periods in the development of the organism.

According to Sullivan, the organism moves from infancy to childhood to the juvenile period, which is marked by the "need for compeers" (51, *p. 227*) that occurs from school entrance to finding a chum; the latter event marks the advent of preadolescence. This stage, ushered in by the appearance of a new type of interest in a person of the same sex, satisfies the need for interpersonal intimacy. Early adolescence, denoted by the emergence of genital interests, blends into late adolescence when the genital interest is patterned (51, *p. 263*). The Sullivan scheme is constructed around the degree of mastery concerning interpersonal relationships which the individual develops in interactive situations prior to and through adolescence. Equally important is Erikson's view that adolescence is the period when identity formation takes firm shape. As Erikson states, ego identity is "the accrued confidence that inner sameness and continuity are matched by the sameness and continuity of one's meanings for others, as evidenced in the tangible promise of a 'career'" (16, *p. 228*). This means that at the completion of adolescence the individual has achieved some degree of harmonious adaptation to his culture and is not beset with excessive doubts and internal conflicts concerning himself and his role in society.

Our view, then, is that development of skills in interpersonal relationships, which fulfill the intimacy needs of the individual and ensure the formation of a socially accepted ego identity, are crucially dependent upon the existence of primary-group relationships with peers in adolescence. As the child is launched from the family into the school groups of childhood and adolescence, the peer groups, especially those of the same sex, begin to assume primacy in the behavior of the child and are of extreme importance in his socialization. In numerous cases the peer groups assume greater subjective meaning for the individual than his family and become the chief influence in his behavior. Under favorable circumstances the traumas and inadequacies of childhood family socialization may be repaired by the primary-group associations with peers.

Peer-Group Participation

In assessing the adolescent socialization experiences of the chronic police case inebriate, the major question involves their participation in peer-group activities as determined by membership in a clique group, a gang, or an intimate friendship group of boys. Group membership at this period is significant for personality development and identity formation. An outstanding student of the role of cliques for human behavior, Allison Davis, has said:

The adolescent's social clique helps him learn those aspects of his identity which his parents cannot conceive and do not know, namely, how one feels, thinks and acts as a social person between childhood and adulthood . . . that is, the clique gives him his one and only chance to behave as an adolescent person, and to secure the group's implicit or explicit interpretation of his behavior. For only his age-group knows what is fair-play or courage, or modesty, or male behavior, or female behavior, and can fortify the adolescent's sense of identity by treating him like one who is adequately fair, courageous, male or female (12, p. 72 f.).

Consistent with this view is the one expounded by Hollingshead:

Sociologically, adolesence is the period in the life of a person when the society in which he functions ceases to regard him (male or female) as a child and does not accord to him full adult status, roles and functions. In terms of behavior it is defined by the roles the person is expected, is allowed to play, is forced to play, or prohibited from playing by virtue of his status in society (24, p. 5).

Adolescence becomes the uneasy journey between secure childhood and the clearly defined status of adulthood. What clarification of status the adolescent achieves must be among his peers. The primary group of age mates accords him status and socializes him to the requisite roles. This brings into focus the importance of adequate adolescent experiences for the inebriate group whose childhood experiences have been shown to be deficient.

Extensive questioning of the inebriates centered around the point of membership in a boys group during adolescence. According to their responses, 28 per cent felt they had been integrated members of a clique group while 72 per cent felt they were never members of any intimate primary same-sex group during the adolescent period. These subjective appraisals may be criticized on the grounds that they do not necessarily represent objective reality. Nevertheless, how the respondent perceived the situation, that is, perceived himself as belonging or isolated during this period, had a dynamic impact on his personality. The significance of this statistic on clique membership can be gauged by comparing the frequency of clique membership among all boys in the Wabash High School, located in St. Louis (Table 26).

Wabash High School draws students from the upper-lower and middle class groups in society, and the incarcerated inebriates are not comparable in class composition and may not be comparable in standards of clique membership, especially in view of the difference in the time periods. However, the general difference between the two groups is highly significant statistically in respect to clique membership: 79 per cent of the students compared to 28 per cent of the future inebriates.

The high incidence of nonparticipation in adolescent clique groups of the same sex by the inebriates is one of the most significant findings of the present investigation. The consequences of this nonpar-

TABLE 26.—*Adolescent Clique Membership of the Sample Compared to Male High-School Students*

| | Sample | | High-School Students[1] | |
	N	%	N	%
Clique members	51	28.2	281	79.2
Nonmembers	130	71.8	74	20.8
*Totals**	*181*	*100.0*	*355*	*100.0*

[1] All male students of Wabash High School, St. Louis, Mo. From Gordon (21).
* Chi squared = 64+; P <.01.

ticipation on personality development requires further exploration.

As has been noted, experience in the primary groups of peers may alleviate traumas incurred in the family of orientation, but this sequel is impossible if group participation does not occur. In Sullivan's personality development scheme a crucial stage, pre-adolescence, centers around the finding of a chum of the same sex with whom the individual forms an intimate bond; this relationship permits the development of situations allowing for the validation of all components of personal worth on the part of each individual to the other. It is in terms of this two-person relationship, the smallest group possible, that one individual develops sensitivity to the needs, desires and aspirations of another person in the environment (16, *pp.* 245–262). In this context are learned the lessons of sharing, of relating significantly to others, and of role expectations. An inadequate development of the self occurred among a significant number of the inebriates because they never experienced the chum relationship.

The lack of intimate primary-group membership at this period has implications for all areas of the personality. The intimate same-sex group functions to reduce the formidable parental authority figures, which the child may have constructed during childhood, by the development of capacity to compare them with the parents of friends and to perceive that parents are in fact humans with foibles as well as strengths. In clique discussions the parental figures are brought into perspective and so need not serve through adulthood as chains which repress the individual. But the adolescent also learns in the clique group that he is similar to others; physically, in terms of the actual joint exploratory activities in the group, which may be a phase of late preadolescence; psychologically, around his needs for intimacy, for acceptance and approval, and for belongingness, which are verbally reciprocated by the significant others; and socially in terms of goals and aspirations and in class beliefs. In the process of learning his similarity to others, anxiety over physical condition, a psychological state, or a social position is substantially lower for the clique member than for the nonmember.

In the warm spontaneous relationships which develop in the group context, the individual finds protection in seeking achievement and success goals based on competition. Anxieties are alleviated, tensions are reduced in the knowledge that his acceptance is built around his unique personality as it is subjectively felt and perceived by the others in the group. The ability to form sustaining group relationships is advantageous to the individual throughout life in the sense that while his emotional resources are dissipated in the pressing situations of occupation and living, his basic resource is the perpetual self-renewal in his group relationships of a primary nature. But the chronic police case inebriates' ability to form sustaining interpersonal relationships is severely limited.

As Allison Davis (12) has noted, the intimate friendship group in adolescence is invaluable in the individual's quest for ego identity. For in the context of the group new identities can be "tried on" and rejected without fear of censure and reprisal from the total society. The person gains the sense of continuity by identification with a structure, the group, larger than himself. But this possibility is denied to people who are isolated and deprived of one of the essential foci for personality development, as is illustrated by the inebriates. These men are unable to relate their personalities to significant others in the environment and find few human outlets for the needs of interpersonal intimacy. The ability to relate is a developmental task for the personality at the stage of adolescence and must be learned at this stage if successful interpersonal relationships are to occur. Failure here leads to a sense of loneliness and isolation from the main stream of society.

In short, the inebriates, as a group deficient in adolescent clique memberships, are unable to relate to significant others. Their incompetence for interpersonal relationships, a consequence of another major source of emotional deprivation, their peers, finds its logical sequel in a lifelong inability to gain emotional support from or fulfill intimacy needs with other individuals.

Adolescence and Heterosexual Participation

In Sullivan's stages of personality development, adolescence is delimited from the emergence of genital desire to its patterning (51, *p. 263*). In "normal" development this patterning is directed toward members of the opposite sex. Ideal development is achieved by the well-oriented adult who is able to fulfill his genital desire as well as his needs for intimacy and security in relationship with the same person of the opposite sex. Thus, one of the major developmental tasks in adolescence is a shift in orientation for the satisfaction of genital needs particularly, but also for intimacy needs, from the same-sex orientation of preadolescence to a cross-sex one in the next stage. As clinical evidence from psychiatry has shown, the shift in personality orientation is not always made to a cross-sex basis in all three areas of intimacy, genitality and security, though it is only when the genital patterning remains same-sex oriented that tremendous conflicts are raised with societal standards and norms.

The inebriates pose many interesting questions in reference to the shift of objects in the fulfillment of their needs in these three areas. Since their preadolescent and adolescent phases are marked by underparticipation in clique groups, with resultant undersocialization, difficulty in shifting to a cross-sex orientation may be anticipated. This expectation is based on the assumption that the clique group serves to support and encourage the individual when he makes his first confused and inept attempts at cross-sex participation. Everyone is making blunders, is confused, or unsure of himself. The peer group members, since they are experiencing the same events, are able to establish an empathic linkage in this area and provide mutual emotional support. But individuals deprived of clique group support, may be thwarted in or precluded from early episodes of cross-sex participation and so may remain handicapped in the subsequent stages.

To assess the shift from same-sex participation, or isolation, to cross-sex orientation, each inebriate was asked to reconstruct his adolescent activities that involved opposite sex members. It was assumed that some degree of cross-sex orientation was in operation if some overt form of a dating pattern for activity in association with girls occurred before the eighteenth birthday. It should be emphasized that nonestablishment of a dating pattern before this age does not indicate the reverse, same-sex orientation. The establishment of a dating pattern is perhaps more indicative of the orientation of the genital needs to a cross-sex basis than of the intimacy needs.

Table 27 reveals that orientation to members of the opposite sex, as reflected in the establishment of a dating pattern before the eighteenth birthday, was the exception rather than the rule among the men in the sample, since two-thirds failed to do so. A more significant pattern emerges if the men are divided by race. This is justified since the Negro offender is usually a cultural drinker whose class position and social background, combined with discrimination, renders him especially vulnerable to arrest and incarceration for offenses that are overlooked, or are not high categoric

TABLE 27.—*Heterosexual Participation During Adolescence, by Race*

	Whites[*]		Negroes[*]		Both Races[*]	
	N	%	N	%	N	%
Established dating pattern	39	28.3	16	50.0	55	32.4
No established dating pattern	99	71.7	16	50.0	115	67.6
Totals	138	100.0	32	100.0	170	100.0

[*] Chi squared for whites versus Negroes = 4.65; P <.05.

risks, in the white population. A comparison of the heterosexual participation of Negro and white offenders reveals a significant difference at the 5 per cent level of confidence. The Negro inebriates show better mastery of the development of heterosexual skills in adolescence than do the whites, and this is related not only to their origin from different cultural groups, but to their different socialization patterns (13). In spite of the statistical difference between the two groups, 50 per cent of the Negroes established no dating pattern during adolescence.

For those who established a pattern of dating during adolescence, a further discrimination was made in reference to the social and psychological significance of the type of pattern. In moving through adolescence, the individual tends to gravitate toward a single dating pattern in contrast to the beginning phase of adolescence which is characterized by group dating, cliques of boys and girls going out together with or without prearranged pairing. In this progression, the preadolescent phase is repeated, the chum of the previous stage being substituted by a member of the opposite sex who can fulfill both genital and intimacy needs in the fully developed heterosexual stage. How far had the inebriates moved on this dating continuum from group participation to paired participation? In 69 per cent of the cases with a dating pattern there was no advance; only in 22 per cent was the end of adolescence characterized by a well-developed pattern of individual dates with one member of the opposite sex, while in the remaining 9 per cent the dating pattern was unstable, in that there was no firmly established paired pattern but there had been movement from group situations.

Given the framework of a developmental scheme of personality, it was hypothesized that unadaptability and lack of success in heterosexual task roles in adolescence should be revealed by the inability to engage in one of the most demanding but at the same time most rewarding interpersonal relationships of adulthood—marriage. Unsuccessful completion of one stage of development

TABLE 28.—*Marital Status, by Heterosexual Participation During Adolescence*

	Single		Ever Married	
	N	%	N	%
Established dating pattern	17	25.4	38	36.9
No established dating pattern	50	74.6	65	63.1
*Totals**	67	100.0	103	100.0

* Chi squared = 1.97; P >.10 <.20.

means that it is difficult to achieve success at a later stage. Table 28 reveals that the general trend of the hypothesis is supported: Individuals who had an established dating pattern during adolescence married more frequently than those who had no established dating pattern. Though the difference is not statistically significant, this hypothesis merits further investigation, particularly with a more refined dating-pattern continuum.

The major conclusion that can be drawn is that the norm for the group was nonparticipation in heterosexual dating patterns during the adolescent phase of development and this is another indication of their undersocialization. Even those who did start a dating pattern tended to stop at group dating and did not advance to individual dating. The inadequacies of these inebriates in building a significant relationship with a member of the opposite sex is reflected in the fact that of all those who ever attempted marriage, 85 per cent are separated or divorced and only 4 per cent are living with their wives.

GOAL ORIENTATIONS DURING ADOLESCENCE

One indication of the progressive movement during adolescence toward socially accepted adult roles is the possession of goals concerning future activity in the occupational and personal areas. Occupational aspirations and personal goals both denote that identity formation is occurring and that the foundation for adult existence is being laid. What occupational and personal goals did the chronic police case inebriates possess? Goals of the middle class, with emphasis on achievement, success orientation, and upward social mobility, were not considered to be suitable criteria in the present group. The major criterion was the individual's possession of ideas and behavior patterns which he felt subjectively directed him toward future events.

Of these men, 35 per cent had possessed specific goals of either a personal or occupational nature during adolescence, while 43 per cent had only goals of a shifting and diffuse nature in terms of providing systematic motivation for the future, and 23 per cent had no goals whatsoever during this period and drifted from situation to situation without any concept of future orientation. In the group with specific goal orientations, many of the goals so rated consisted of an overwhelming desire to escape from an unbearable home situation, or the ambition to make one's way as an independent unit to escape the monotony of community routine. Whether these aims should have been scored positively is debatable. A specific orientation at the end of adolescence, which is usual in adequately socialized individuals, was the exception for this group.

In Chapter 4 the inadequacy of the families of orientation of these inebriates as agents of socialization was demonstrated. As a check of this factor, an attempt was made to assess the role of their families in the formation of the life goals of these men. The family of orientation was the sole determining influence for life goals, according to the men, in 13 per cent of the cases, and a partial determinant in another 34 per cent, while in 48 per cent the family played no significant role in this respect and in 5 per cent no family unit was in operation. These results are based on 171 cases. The inability of the family to provide even partially acceptable goal models for these men is another index of their undersocialization.

ADOLESCENCE AND ALCOHOL

Adolescence in American society is generally the time when the individual has his first exposure to alcoholic beverages, although there are exceptions to this in certain cultural groups. Basic attitudes and psychological reactions to alcohol in reference to problem situations begin to be established.

Each subject was asked when he began drinking, and the results are presented in Table 29. Age when drinking begins is different from first contact with alcoholic beverages, which may occur earlier. Table 29 further presents data on age at which drinking began for 50 male alcoholism clinic patients and 50 male workhouse inmates studied by Feeney and his associates (17) in Washington, D. C. There appear to be no statistically significant differences in the ages at onset of drinking among the three groups with comparable median ages. Among the incarcerated inebriates 68 per cent had begun drinking by their twenty-first birthday, 19 per cent began

TABLE 29.—*Age when Drinking Began for Three Groups of Problem Drinkers*

Age (years)	Present Sample		Male Workhouse Inmates[1]		Male Clinic Patients[1]	
	N	%	N	%	N	%
12 or under	2	1.0	0	0	1	2.0
13–15	12	6.4	6	12.0	7	14.0
16–20	113	60.4	24	48.0	30	60.0
21–25	36	19.3	11	24.0	11	22.0
Over 25	14	7.5	4	8.0	1	2.0
Unknown	10	5.4	4	8.0	0	0
Totals	187	100.0	50	100.0	50	100.0

[1] From Feeney and associates (17).

between their twenty-first and twenty-fifth years, and 8 per cent after 25 years of age, while 5 per cent could not remember this datum. The range for the age of onset of drinking is quite large, from 7 in the youngest case to 35 in the oldest. The heaviest concentration occurs in the late adolescent years of 16, 17 and 18, which account for 44 per cent.[2] Age, however, can hardly be as crucial a factor in determining whether an individual will become a problem drinker as the contexts of the early drinking situations as they relate to his personality characteristics.

In 54 per cent of the present sample the early drinking experiences were with other boys or teen-agers, but not necessarily with fellow members of a clique or close friendship group. In many cases the other boys were casual acquaintances, or socially acceptable only in the sense that they met the criterion of someone with whom to interact. A small number did have their first drinking experiences with a clique, but since the majority of the inebriates were not clique members in this phase of development, the possibilities of this pattern were limited. For 25 per cent the early drinking experiences were with adults who were not members of the family. Here chance seems to be more significant in the selection of a drinking

[2] In this connection it is interesting to note Ullman's (60) attempt to relate first drinking experiences with inebriety. In a sample of 143 inmates of a county House of Correction (in Massachusetts) with "a pattern of addictive drinking" he found that of those who remembered their first drink (nine-tenths of the sample) 47 per cent had then been between 15 and 19 years of age and 37 per cent 20 years and over. In a sample of male college students, however, 63 per cent were between 15 and 19, and only 3 per cent 20 years or older at their first drink. The remainder in both samples were 14 years of age or younger at the time of their first drink, and the difference between the groups if analyzed at the age 15 breakpoint is statistically highly significant. These findings, however, do not lend themselves to comparison with ours because of the "first drink" criterion in Ullman's study.

partner, since many of the men in this subgroup were moving about and could have only casual and temporary acquaintances as drinking companions. Only 6 per cent of the future police case inebriates began their early drinking at home with family approval. Other situational contexts which predominantly involve drinking alone at a bar, or in secret from the family, accounted for 14 per cent of the cases.

What significance may be attached to the general situational contexts in which the early drinking experiences of these men occurred? First, the largest number had their earliest drinking experiences in a social group or with chance acquaintances. Given the physiological, psychological and cultural functions of alcohol, it can be hypothesized, although this proposition was not tested, that the early drinking situations provided the undersocialized, emotionally deprived individuals with interaction episodes which they were capable of handling with their limited skills in interpersonal relationships. The drinking situation is less demanding of interpersonal skills, and alcohol depresses the activities and anxieties which are thought to be mediated by the frontal lobe of the cerebral cortex. The psychological reaction of the future inebriate to the early drinking episodes could indeed have been a favorable one, associated with a fulfillment of intimacy needs and a gain of emotional supports on a level with which he was able to cope and occurring in a sociocultural context that could be capitalized on at every bar and tavern. In other words, drinking situations for the future chronic inebriate were rewarding experiences in the emotional sense and, at first, the physiological sense, but undemanding in the social and cultural realm. With his limited skill for interpersonal relationships and his lack of secondary skills in an occupational or educational sense, the drinking situation was one in which he could subjectively view himself as competent, skillful and resourceful.[3]

---

[3] These ideas are in agreement with the findings of Ullman (60) in a group of addictive drinkers interviewed in a Massachusetts county House of Correction. In comparison with a group of much younger college students, more of the inebriates remembered their first drink, had it in the company of others than family members and elsewhere than in a private home or regular drinking place, and became intoxicated in some degree. In spite of sampling problems which do not allow conclusive interpretations, Ullman's findings at least suggest that for the future inebriates the first drinking experience was heavily laden emotionally with relatively high ego involvement, and that these men subsequently found it rewarding to be able to "drink like a man."

Inquiry was also made concerning the attitudes of the parents toward the subjects' early drinking. There are cases both of approval and disapproval, and any facile explanation of drinking behavior based on parental attitudes toward alcohol should be rejected as an oversimplification. In 12 per cent (based on 171 cases) both parents are said to have approved of drinking by the son while in 38 per cent both parents are reported to have disapproved. In 11 per cent the father approved while the mother disapproved. In one case the mother approved while the father disapproved. The approval of the parents could not be assessed in 38 per cent because the family was not intact or drinking began after the son left the family. The role of the family in the drinking behavior of the individual does not appear to be important on the overt level of approval or disapproval as dichotomous choices, but exercises its major importance in the cultural patterns the family transmits to the child in the socialization period, and in the quality and quantity of socialization experiences provided for his basic social and psychological needs. The family provides the cultural context within which the perception of alcoholic beverages occurs and provides guideposts concerning the situations in which drinking behavior is or is not proper.

ADOLESCENT ADJUSTMENT

A major thesis of this study is that the chronic police case inebriate is undersocialized, as determined by both qualitative and quantitative indexes in the family of orientation and in the adolescent sphere of development. In summary of the adolescent phase of development, two measures were used to portray the adjustment of these men. One (the subjective index) is the inebriate's characterization of himself during his adolescence; the other is an index of adjustment constructed from the interview data.

The subjective index was built on questions the interviewer posed to the inebriate concerning his adolescence. Each respondent was asked to give a descriptive picture of himself while he was a teenager. The crucial thing about this portrayal is not whether another observer would characterize the inebriate as he did himself, but the fact that this picture represented the self-image to which the individual was reacting. The portrayals were divided into the following four major categories: 42 per cent characterized themselves as shy, timid, or having difficulty in making friends; 39 per cent felt that they were aggressive, "cocky" or "pushy" individuals with little consideration for the rights of others; 6 per cent used terms to indicate a sullen, resentful, negative attitude of personality during this period; and 13 per cent characterized themselves in other terms, indicating mainly a healthy and well-adjusted orientation (without problems) in reference to themselves during this period. In self-characterizations, though they are subject to the distortions of selective memory and recall, the noticeable thing is the large proportion who indicate problems of interpersonal relationships. Timidity and shyness are overt manifestations of the difficulties involved in the inability to form satisfying and rewarding relationships with significant others. Aggressiveness and "cockiness" are symbolic of the inability to maintain relationships in the interpersonal sphere. Undersocialization, beginning in the family and continuing in the peer groups, is evidenced in the reflected self-appraisals which the inebriates present of themselves in their adolescence.

A more objective index to evaluate adolescent socialization experience and the significance of these situations for positive identity formation was constructed by the following criteria: (a) participation in a clique or close friendship group of boys, (b) heterosexual participation as reflected in an established dating pattern, (c) existence of goals and aspirations, whether of a middle-class nature or not, (d) family integration as reflected in the individual's sense of belonging to the family unit, and (e) positive school adaptation as reflected in attendance and performance. If all these factors were found in the case, the socialization experience was scored as good or above average; four present was scored adequate or average, and three or fewer was rated as poor or below what would be desirable for adequate socialization. This rating policy can be defended on the grounds that all five factors are highly desirable for ideal socialization. The individual can make an adequate adjustment with the absence of one factor because of the favorableness of the others, but serious doubt must be entertained about the adjustment level when any two of the five factors are lacking.

The results of this classification indicated that the symptoms which warn of difficulties in assuming adult social roles are already present in these men at the end of the adolescent development era. By the index of adolescent adjustment, 86 per cent of our sample were rated poor; only 10 per cent could be rated adequate or average, while in 4 per cent the index could not be applied because of incomplete data. In only one case were all five factors present.

SUMMARY

A summary statement of the adolescent socialization experiences of the chronic police case inebriates is inherent in the results of the index of adolescent adjustment, on which 86 per cent were rated poor or inadequate. The opportunity for removing or ameliorating the negative depriving experiences in the families of orientation was lost in the barrenness of the adolescent socialization events. Deprivation in basic social and psychological needs at adolescence occurred in a personality framework already deprived of warm, spontaneous primary-group relationships. The consequences of the inadequacies of primary-group experiences will be expressed in the inability of these men to handle secondary roles relating to occupational and educational tasks and primary roles in the marital situation.

Chapter 6

EXPERIENCES IN SECONDARY TASK ROLES

THE QUALITY and to some extent the quantity of the socialization experiences of the chronic police case inebriates in their families of orientation and in adolescent peer groups were described in Chapters 4 and 5. These primary groups function vitally in the personality development of the individual by providing for the fulfillment of fundamental needs such as security, response, recognition and emotional support. Furthermore, the individual's continued relation to primary groups provides channels for the release of anxiety in crises. Primary-group associations proliferate for the individual as he develops competence in interpersonal relationships and is able effectively to relate himself psychologically, as well as socially, to another individual. The achievement of tasks that center around the ability to relate to others and form new primary-group associations are the primary task roles.

There are present in society secondary task roles which call for achievement under demanding situations, such as the performance of educational roles in childhood, adolescence and early adulthood, occupational roles in adulthood, and marital roles at maturity. These secondary roles demand, and their successful execution by the individual are built upon, a high degree of competence in primary-group associations. Some confusion is perhaps engendered by the inclusion of marital roles as secondary roles, but the emphasis here is not only on marriage as an interpersonal relationship but also on the role demands on father as breadwinner.

It is our hypothesis that the lack of experience in primary task roles on the part of the incarcerated inebriates and their ineptness in interpersonal relations will render them unable to perform satisfactorily in the demanding achievement situations connected with educational, occupational and marital roles.

EDUCATIONAL ROLES

The educational attainment of the inebriates has been discussed previously (Table 9, Chapter 2), and it should be restated that the educational level of the group is extremely low in that 73 per cent have an 8th-grade education or less, only six ever attended college, and only one finished college. Thus the possible impact of the school structure on the personality of these men is not great. Given the predominantly lower-class level of the group, education was not likely to be highly evaluated in their families.

Although other factors than low competence in primary task roles operate to explain the school adaptation of the inebriates, it is possible to investigate their level of adaptation in reference to formal educational roles by three measures: (a) participation in school activities, (b) truancy, and (c) expulsion from school.

Participation in school activities is indicative of the degree of the individual's integration into the formal and informal structures of the school system. That the inebriates were not well integrated is obvious from the fact that 89 per cent of 126 cases did not participate. The attrition in the number of cases here is due primarily to the large number who left school in the elementary grades where extracurricular activities play a relatively insignificant role. Truancy from school is considered by psychologists to indicate fundamental problems of the personality; it may safely be considered as symptomatic of the child's inability to meet his needs in the school system. Of 157 cases, 33 per cent reported themselves as frequently truant from school. It is of great interest to note that this type of adjustment was used as a pattern of flight from the problems of the school situation rather than more aggressive forms of behavior which might lead to expulsion. Only 7 of the future inebriates were expelled from school, a proportion perhaps not far from average. Thus the school adaptation of these men was marked by passivity both in their inability to participate in activities and in their recourse to truancy instead of aggressive behavior in the face of difficult situations.

Since it was known that the majority of them had not finished their schooling, the men were asked why they left school. The most frequently stated reason (47 per cent) was phrased in terms of economic necessity, of having had to go to work to help support himself or his family. It should be noted that cases of leaving school to work without a problem of economic necessity have not been included in the preceding category, which thus reflects as nearly as possible the fact that nearly half of these men left school because of the pressures of sheer existence, in harmony with their class level in society. Another 15 per cent quit because of an intense dislike of school, and 2 per cent because of academic failure. A multitude of miscellaneous reasons was given by 26 per cent, many of which appear to be flimsily covered rationalizations for the basic fact of dissatisfaction. Only 10 per cent left on graduation from high school or college. Thus the two primary causes involved in school discontinuance were (a) the external factor of economic necessity deriving from class position; and (b) the internal factor of inability to perform in the demanding situations, both interpersonal and achievement based, that occur in the school system.

The role of the family in the individual's leaving school was assessed by inquiring concerning the reaction of the family to the event. The responses demonstrate that the parents of these inebriates were not particularly potent forces in engendering motivation to continue schooling. In 12 per cent of the cases the families encouraged the child to quit school, primarily for economic need, while in almost half, 47 per cent, the families approved the decision made by the boy. In 11 per cent the families did not care whether the boy quit or continued. Thus in 70 per cent of the cases the family acquiesced in the child's leaving school. A conflict between the wishes of the parents and the son's decision to leave school occurred in 16 per cent of the cases, with resulting overt antagonism in just two instances. The remaining 14 per cent of the inebriates graduated at least from high school.

The school adjustment of the inebriates was poor in terms of their low educational achievement. Their leaving school can be attributed to three major factors which overlap to a certain extent. First, they belonged to families which did not place a high value on formal education. Second, their earnings were needed to help support themselves or their families. Third, their low competence for meeting the demands of the school situation rendered attendance disagreeable.

OCCUPATIONAL ROLES

A comparison (Chapter 2, Table 10) of the occupational distribution of the incarcerated inebriates according to primary skills with those of males in the labor force in Monroe County showed significant differences between the two groups, the inebriates being overrepresented in unskilled occupations and underrepresented in the professional, managerial, sales and clerical categories.

In the present section the adult occupational experiences of the inebriates will be considered, with the greatest emphasis upon work activities in the year previous to their incarceration. In essence, the focus is on the development of the career pattern of the individual as it is reflected in the occupational sphere, and on how he has handled the demanding occupational roles in the culture.

The chronic police case inebriates as a group are characterized by a lack of systematic training which would have prepared them for the occupational roles which an adult member of society is expected to perform. This is partly reflected in their low educational attainment, but might have been balanced by technical or occupational training. Only 31 per cent of these men ever received apprenticeship direction or on-the-job training. Technical school training is claimed by 3 per cent, other forms of occupational training were received by another 3 per cent, and one man went to a military service training school. The remaining 63 per cent never received any sort of job technical training. The inebriates in the labor market really have only their hands to bargain with in an attempt to secure employment.

In order to determine the extent to which those men who did possess primary occupational skills of a more specialized nature had been working in occupations reflecting these abilities, an occupational chronology was established for each subject and the time since he was employed in his primary occupational skill was recorded. Based on 166 cases, 50 per cent had been employed at their primary occupation less than 6 months before incarceration. These results are slightly misleading, however, since the sample contained a large number of individuals whose occupational skills were of such a low order that, unless unemployed, they hardly could be working below their level. This group of 50 per cent contains the relatively frequent category of unskilled workers. Another 2 per cent reported having been employed in their primary occupational skill within 6 months to 1 year before incarceration, but in 13 per cent it was 1 to 3 years, in 19 per cent 3 to 10 years, and in 16 per cent over 10 years since they had worked at their primary occupations.

In viewing the occupational profile of these men, job stability is a crucial index of their present level of adjustment. This was evaluated on the basis of several components: (a) number of jobs held in the year preceding the present incarceration, (b) duration of the last job, (c) duration of the longest job in the individual's occupational history, (d) time since employed before the present incarceration, and (*e*) number of weeks employed in the year prior to incarceration. These indexes allow us to compare the present occupational stability of the group with the period of greatest stability in their career and, furthermore, to compare this group occupationally with other groups possessing a drinking problem.

A comparison of number of jobs held in the year before incarceration between the present sample and Bacon's (3) arrested inebriates reveals a statistically highly significant difference in the number who held only one job during that time (Table 30). It should be noted that both groups have median ages in the forties and thus should not be differentiated in this respect because of age.

Perhaps no better indication of the occupational instability of the incarcerated inebriates can be found than in the length of time they were employed on their most recent job. This information, obtained in 171 cases, showed that the duration of the last job held by 26 per cent was only 1 day; it was 2 to 7 days for 22 per cent, 8 to 30 days for 20 per cent, 31 to 90 days for 16 per cent, 91 to 180 days for 6 per cent, 181 days to 1 year for 5 per cent, 1 to 3 years for 4 per cent, and 3 years or more for only 1 per cent. In this respect the incarcerated inebriates are decidedly unlike the patients seen in alcoholism clinics as reported by Straus and Bacon (49). The latter showed evidence of comparatively high occupational stability as measured by the duration of the most recent steady job, which was 1 year or more in 75 per cent compared to 5 per cent in the present sample. This difference between the two groups is statistically significant at the 1 per cent level by chi-squared test. Present occupational stability seems to be one

TABLE 30.—*Number of Jobs Held During Year Before Present Incarceration by Two Samples of Inebriates* (*in Per Cent*)

	Present Sample	Arrested Inebriates[1]
1	13.6*	35.9*
2	9.5	26.0
3	8.9	13.7
4 or more	39.0	16.3
Unemployed or odd jobs[2]	29.0	7.5
Separate contracting	0	0.6
Totals	*100.0*	*100.0*

[1] Men arrested for intoxication in five Connecticut cities in 1942. Source: Bacon (3, p. 24).

[2] Bacon's classification contains only the category "odd jobs" while in the present study the unemployed and odd-job holders were combined.

* Chi squared = 31+; P <.01.

characteristic which sharply differentiates the arrested inebriate from the incarcerated inebriate, and the alcoholism clinic patient from the incarcerated inebriate.

The level of occupational integration of the incarcerated inebriates was assayed also in terms of the longest job experience in the individual's occupational chronology. This presented a difficult problem owing to the nature of certain occupations. The sample included many railroad workers ("gandy dancers"), merchant seamen and construction laborers. These occupations may involve mobility without necessarily evidencing instability. For example, the merchant seaman may change ships frequently in the course of his career without being occupationally unstable. In these cases the longest period of consecutive time spent in steady merchant seaman activities or steady railroad "gandy dancer" work has been recorded as one job experience. This biases the determination of the longest period of steady employment toward an overestimation of job stability. This reservation should be kept in mind in examining the comparison (Table 31) between the incarcerated inebriates by age categories and the alcoholism clinic patients surveyed by Straus and Bacon (49).

In comparing the duration of the longest job experience of the clinic patients and the incarcerated inebriates, the age differential between the two groups will have a bearing on the results. The clinic group has a mean age of 41.2 years and only 19 per cent are 50 years or older, while the mean age of the incarcerated inebriates is 47.7 and 45 per cent are 50 years or older. Moreover, many of the clinic patients were still employed at their longest job compared to only two inebriates who were employed at their most

TABLE 31.—*Duration of Longest Job Experience of Present Sample and of Alcoholism Clinic Patients, by Major Age Categories (in Per Cent)*

Duration (years)	PRESENT SAMPLE			1,540 Alcoholism Clinic Patients[1]
	Under 45	45 and Over	All Ages	
Less than 1	19.7	11.2	14.3	8
1–3	9.8	6.5	7.7	18
3–10	57.4	36.5	44.1	41
10–20	13.1	38.3	29.1	22
20 and over	0	7.5	4.8	11
Totals	100.0	100.0	100.0	100

[1] From Straus and Bacon (49, p. 251).

recent jobs 3 years or more before they were incarcerated. Given these major reservations, differences do appear between the two groups in reference to duration of longest job experience, especially at the extremes of the distribution. The longest job experience of 14 per cent of the incarcerated inebriates was less than 1 year, while only 8 per cent of the clinic patients fell into this category. The difference is more pronounced if the former are divided into two major age categories. Of those less than 45 years old, 20 per cent have had no job lasting a year, compared to 11 per cent of those 45 years of age and over. A total of 5 per cent of the incarcerated inebriates have held a job for 20 years or more, compared to 11 per cent of the clinic patients.

We are dealing with a bimodal distribution of the inebriates in reference to occupational stability. Among those who are 45 years of age and over, 8 per cent had held one job 20 or more years, and 38 per cent had been employed from 10 to 20 years in one job; it should be noted, however, that this pattern of occupational stability no longer exists. Among those 45 years and older, 18 per cent have never held the same job for as long as 3 years. In actuality, the older group and to a lesser extent the younger group are marked by the presence of two divergent subgroups in reference to occupational stability: one of these reflects occupational stability at an earlier period, particularly before they reached 45 years of age, when occupational disintegration began, the other, at all age levels, has never evidenced any degree of occupational stability.

The next index of occupational stability is the length of time between last employment and present incarceration. Based on 164 cases, these times were 2 to 7 days for 33 per cent, 8 to 30 days for 13 per cent, 31 to 90 days for 8 per cent, 91 to 180 days for 6 per cent, 181 days to 1 year for 9 per cent, 1 to 3 years for 7 per cent, and 3 years or longer for 3 per cent. Thus 21 per cent had been working on the day of the arrest leading to the present incarceration, 67 per cent had been employed within a month, 81 per cent within 6 months, and 90 per cent within a year.

The final index of occupational stability is the number of weeks the men worked in the year prior to their present incarceration. Of those reporting this item (131 cases), one-third had not worked as much as a week; 17 per cent had worked from 1 to 10 weeks, and only 8 per cent had worked a total of 41 to 52 weeks during the previous year. Since jobs are plentiful, it is obvious that most of these men had reached an extreme point of occupational deterioration. As was hypothesized, nearly all the chronic police case inebriates were not self-supporting before being jailed and were unsuccessful in the performance of secondary task roles.

The scantiness of their total yearly employment, when coupled with their average hourly wage scales, gives a bleak picture of the economic status of these men. On their last jobs, 11 per cent were receiving $0.75 an hour or less, while 25 per cent received between $0.76 and $1 an hour. The most frequent salary scale was between $1.01 and $1.50 an hour, reported by 49 per cent, while only 4 per cent reported earning more than $2 an hour. These wage scales, even with full-time employment, would provide little more than bare subsistence for the majority.

The incarcerated inebriates are characterized by extremes of occupational instability and deterioration. This was reflected in the number of jobs held in the year preceding incarceration, in the duration of the last job, in the time since last employed, and in the number of weeks employed in the year prior to incarceration. That this condition has not always prevailed for all these men is suggested by the data (Table 31) on duration of the longest job experience in the life career. Many have been occupationally stable at some point in the past. As a summary of this particular point, a characteristic job classification for the sample group prior to incarceration was constructed. This shows that 73 per cent of the men are employed as casual or seasonal laborers and 16 per cent are mostly unemployed due either to physical or mental deterioration and constant penal incarcerations. Only one man was classified as self-employed, while 9 per cent of the men evidenced a pattern of steady employment. In all, the occupational level of the group at present is extremely marginal and has developed to this status over a long time sequence.

The marginality of the group in the occupational sphere is reflected in the following case history:

Case 10. John O'Hara came to this country from rural Ireland 29 years ago, at the age of 20. Since the age of 8 years John had been working to help support his family on their government-owned farm. Mr. O'Hara was a cripple, and all the children had to work the farm. When John was 12, his father died, and Mrs. O'Hara went out to work in a grocery store. Although financially troubled, the family remained a cooperative unit, and John remembers his home as friendly, warm and comfortable.

By the time John was 20 his brothers and sisters were marrying and settling down in Eire. John developed a wanderlust. He heard about the opportunities in the United States and set out to improve his lot in that country.

The following year, in Massachusetts, he got a job doing brass and copper tubing. This lasted 3 years, until the depression came. During the next 5 years he had a very hard time finding work but managed to get some seasonal work at resort hotels. He was terribly lonely. He had considered marrying, before the depression, but the "hard times" changed his mind. In 1934, when he was 30, he started to drink.

John began working on the railroad in 1938, and liked it. But after 5 years he abandoned railroad work and hired out as a farm laborer. This, too, lasted 5 years. Since then he has worked at whatever he could find, which has not been much. He is too old now for the job he prefers, railroad work. They do not hire men over 45. He tried being a hospital attendant for 8 months and says he likes live-in jobs. In the past year he worked 6 months, in a cannery and on a farm.

John likes people and is pleasant, polite, alert and in good health. (The interviewer stated that he would not classify John as a chronic alcoholic, and that, given a more rewarding environment, John would "give a good account of himself.") He has been arrested for public intoxication 12 times in the past 12 years. He drinks with other men, in bouts that last 2 or 3 days. John points out that a single man like himself, with his background, usually ends up in some bar getting his comfort out of a bottle.

The inebriates as a group, judged by the dominant middle-class values in American society, have become occupational failures and have been unable to achieve under the demanding conditions which this secondary task role involves. A consideration of the occupational chronology as it relates to the drinking pattern of the individual will be presented later.

MARITAL ROLES

It is our hypothesis that experience in the primary groups of family and peers leads to competence in handling interpersonal relationships, and that this makes itself felt in the adult phase of life in the ability to handle secondary task roles. Interactive episodes and experiences which occurred before adulthood have a profound effect on the ability to perform marital roles. In Chapter 5 we considered the dating and courtship complex of the inebriates and the influence of intimate friendship groups on their behavior. In the present section the concern is with performance of the chronic police case inebriates in the marital roles as determined by the stability of their marriages.

As has been previously noted (Chapter 2, Table 6), this group of inebriates contains a disproportionately large number of men (41 per cent) who had never married, but 59 per cent (110 men) did marry, and it is with this group that we are concerned here.

Certain basic facts concerning the marriages of these men are immediately pertinent: 95 have been married only once and 15 twice. Not one reported having married a third time. The fertility of the marriages is rather low. No children were reported by 26 per cent,[1] 44 per cent reported only 1 or 2 children, and at the opposite end of the continuum 11 per cent reported having had 5 or more children. The median number of children for the inebriates who ever married was 1.25.

Since the marriages of the inebriates have in almost all cases been broken by divorce, desertion or death, a relevant question is the duration of the marriages. This information is available in 102 cases. In 1 per cent the duration was less than 6 months; in 8 per cent, 6 months to 1 year; in 27 per cent, 1 to 3 years; in 28 per cent 3 to 10 years; in 28 per cent more, 10 to 20 years; and in 9 per cent, 20 years or longer.[2] Thus marriages which lasted less than 3 years characterize slightly over one-third of the inebriates who married, but there are almost as many who were married between 10 and 20 years, and nearly 1 in 10 stayed married 20 or more years. A contrasting pattern of marital stability is obtained, as in the case of occupational stability.

Evidence that marital stability was characteristic of an earlier period in the life history of the incarcerated inebriates was obtained by inquiring when they had their last contact (not necessarily in the marital union) with their wives. The responses (Table 32) indicate that contact with the wife and any integrating features that she might bring to the inebriate's situation are not factors of primary importance at the present moment. At least 10 years had elapsed since 70 per cent of the men 45 years of age and over had their last contact with their wives and between 5 and 10

[1] Kiser and Whelpton (30), who studied 6,551 Indianapolis native white couples whose fertility period was almost complete, reported that 19 per cent of the wives had no children. Of course, these two samples are not comparable, since the Indianapolis group represents many different subcultural segments of the urban environment.

[2] In the four cases married and living with spouse, the duration of the marriage was taken as of the time of the interview.

TABLE 32.—*Time Since Last Contact with Wife, by Age Categories*

Last Contact (years)	Under 45 Years		45 Years and Over		All Ages	
	N	%	N	%	N	%
Less than 1	13	31.7	5	7.8	18	17.1
1–3	5	12.2	2	3.1	7	6.7
3–5	2	4.9	3	4.7	5	4.8
5–10	12	29.2	9	14.1	21	20.0
10 or more	9	22.0	45	70.3	54	51.4
Totals	*41*	*100.0*	*64*	*100.0*	*105*	*100.0*

years in another 14 per cent. Only 8 per cent of these older men had been in contact with their wives in the past year. Of the men under 45 years of age, 32 per cent had been in contact with their wives in the past year but the majority, 51 per cent, not within 5 years. In the total sample, three out of four had not communicated with their wives in the past 3 years. This leads to the general conclusion that there is little possibility that a reintegration of the family structure will occur for those who are married but separated, and that as these inebriates grow older their contacts with their former spouses will be increasingly distant.

Further information on marital roles, particularly that related to parenthood, was gained by asking each man concerning the last contact with any of his children. Recent contact between father and child is atypical. Only 14 per cent (of 80 cases) reported having been in communication with a child within 3 months prior to the present incarceration. In 35 per cent the last such contact had occurred 10 or more years ago, and in another 23 per cent between 5 and 10 years ago. More than three-fourths of those who were fathers had not been in communication with their offspring in the last year. This fact graphically illustrates the nonintegration of these inebriates in a relationship which is considered one of the most sacred in the society, and one for which the maximum inculcation of duty and responsibility is engendered. In his downward spiral the chronic police case inebriate has abdicated one of the most obligatory relationships, in both the social and psychological sense, in the society.

From the interview data it is possible to review in some detail the marital role performances of those men who reported a married and living with spouse status; those who reported a married but separated or divorced status; and those who reported a single status. The last group has never assumed a marital status but this does not mean that they should be ignored in a general consideration of marital roles.

Only 4 of the 187 inebriates reported a married and living with spouse status at the time of the interview. All of these men were under 45 years of age. All reported that at one time in their marital history they had been temporarily separated from their wives. From the case data it is safe to assume that their present marital adjustment is marked by extreme discord. The present jail sentence has created greater friction in the husband–wife relationship according to all the respondents. Three of these men stated that their drinking behavior was the precipitating factor in their previous separations from their wives. At the time of the husbands' incarceration, 3 wives were dependent upon welfare grants for their support; the fourth was working. One would predict that in all these cases the marriage is near dissolution, and that if the husband's drinking problem is not resolved, the relationship will be severed entirely.

The men who reported a separated or divorced status were asked concerning the role of their drinking behavior in the break-up of the marriage. Four out of 5 felt that their excessive drinking was a crucial factor, while the remainder felt that their use of alcoholic beverages had not been important. These proportions may not be accepted without reservation, since drinking behavior may be only the verbalized explanation which hides the dynamic psychological and social factors involved in the marital histories. Divorce and separation were viewed by 83 per cent of the inebriates (76 men) as marking a point after which they drank excessively with greater intensity and frequency, while 17 per cent (16 men) felt that they did not drink more after separation or divorce. As will be noted further in Chapter 7, the inability to perform the demanding task roles involved in marriage and subsequent divorce or separation creates a crisis situation. One avenue open to some individuals for confronting the crisis is increased recourse to alcohol. The data indicate that this may have occurred frequently among these men.

When questioned as to whether they might marry again, 9 per cent, chiefly in the younger age brackets, replied affirmatively but 91 per cent of these separated or divorced men had no desire to remarry. In fact, their life now is marked by only sporadic contacts with members of the opposite sex. The majority, 66 per cent, have no type of intimate relations with females at the present time, and 28 per cent state that their contacts with women are limited to occasional casual "pick-ups" or "semi-pros," sought only for the gratification of physical sexual needs and without reference to intimacy needs. A small number of men, 7 per cent, state that their contacts with women follow the cultural pattern of dating with more or less steady friends. Little physical or psychological energy is expended by the divorced–separated group in social contacts with members of the opposite sex. On the overt plane, as a group, they display little interest in the opposite sex.[3]

Another indication of the general level of distinterest on the part of these inebriates in the opposite sex is obtained from their preferences in drinking companions. Since drinking and behavior associated with it dominate the lives of these men and compose almost all their activities, this item is perhaps the most revealing index of their interaction preferences.

The separated and divorced inebriates strongly favor a group situation when drinking, since only 9 per cent prefer to drink by themselves. They are male oriented in that 80 per cent prefer to drink in the company of men, while only 6 per cent prefer drinking with women. Preference for mixed company accounted for the remaining 5 per cent.

It is extremely significant that 41 per cent of the men in the entire sample have never married, and this fact has been commented on in Chapter 2. Although it was beyond the province of the present investigation to explore the reasons for this high incidence of non-marriage, a general effort was made to determine the attitudes of the "single" men (i.e., those who reported they had never married) toward assuming the marital role. First, these men were asked whether at any time during their life they had considered marriage. Thirty men (43 per cent of those responding) stated that they had at some time considered marriage; the remainder claimed that they had never contemplated it. They were asked also whether at the present time they thought they might ever marry. Only 6 men (9 per cent) answered affirmatively; these men were generally less than 35 years of age. The others denied any possibility of marriage in the future. However he may have felt at an earlier period in his life cycle, the chronic police case inebriate is not oriented toward an assumption of the marital role at the present stage in his career.

[3] It is interesting to note that from a review of the psychiatric case records of 63 male patients in an alcoholism clinic, Levine (32, *p. 680*) concluded that "a decided majority . . . showed a diminished interest in heterosexual relationships."

The cross-sex orientation of these men is extremely weak. When asked if they had any women friends before they were incarcerated, the majority replied in the negative: 68 per cent had no female contacts indicating cross-sex orientation, and 32 per cent had female contacts ranging on the continuum from a steady dating pattern by a few of the younger men to casual relationships with "semi-pros" by some of the older men. But their disinterest in members of the opposite sex is not, from the data available, marked by the reverse, same-sex orientation. It appears, rather, that the middle-aged and older inebriates are almost asexual in their orientation; and that because the expenditure of physical and psychological energy in maintaining the drinking pattern is so extensive, they have little interest for activities outside this sphere.

The following case histories illustrate marital role performances: one of marriage marked by failure, the other of never assuming the marital role.

Case 11. Jack LaFever has lived in Rochester ever since he was born, 38 years ago. Jack's father, of French-Canadian parents, was steadily employed as a brass molder. His mother came from Canada. Mr. and Mrs. LaFever had five daughters and one son, Jack. Jack states that his parents were "in love more than average," but the family as a whole did not share activities. Rarely together, they never went to church. Mr. LaFever was a Catholic, his wife a Protestant.

As the only son, Jack was close to his father. Nevertheless, he states that his father never taught him how to do things, like sports or chores. He "learned by himself." Jack had a newspaper route and evidently this kept him busy. He did not contribute to the family by helping with the chores and he received no discipline at home. He believes that there were "average" good relations in the family.

Jack discontinued his schooling after grade school because he was "too nervous and couldn't sit still." He found it hard to read because he had hurt his right eye. He did poorly in his studies and was often a truant. Jack's family did not seem to care that he left school. He had taken no part in school activities but was the leader of his gang, which played ball together.

Jack received no technical job training. As a youth he had wanted to be a mechanic, "because of the money." His first job lasted 6 months. His longest job, over 3 years, was in a foundry. Later he spent 2 years with the railroad as an iron worker. He tried the Civilian Conservation Corps for just 1 day. Now he seems to be unable to work for anyone for any length of time. He works periodically as a mover and has installed oil burners for two seasons.

Jack dated girls frequently before he was 18, and married at the age of 19. The marriage was ill-fated from the beginning. They separated periodically, and Jack has spent three terms in jail for assaulting his wife. Jack "started drinking" when he was 21 and he calls his wife a "no good drunkard." They have five children, now dependent on public support, to whom Jack is completely indifferent. His 15-year-old daughter is confined to a state institution as a wayward minor. Jack says he met her on the street shortly before she was arrested. She was wandering around with several boys, was in possession of marijuana cigarettes and told her father she was running away from home. He tells this story casually, as if it had happened to someone else.

Jack obtained a divorce a year ago, and this means to him the freedom to marry his current "sweetheart." He expresses no regrets about his broken family, feels no responsibility toward its members, and contributes nothing to their financial support. He blames everything on his wife who, he says, is "filthy" (a poor housekeeper, untidy, slovenly), a "good for nothing drunk," and "promiscuous." (Jack says she has been living with another man for several years.) He is anxious to marry his "girl friend," who is now in the process of getting a divorce. They go drinking together and he talks of the "good times we'll have together."

Jack has been arrested 11 times in all; 6 arrests on the charge of public intoxication; 3 for assault on his wife; 1 for driving without an operator's license; and 1 for leaving the scene of an accident.

The interviewer characterized Jack as "loud, rough, crude, boastful and aggressive to the point of being obnoxious."

Case 12. Fred Baker remembers his parents only vaguely, since they died when he was 10 years old. Mr. Baker, the father of nine children, was a tenant farmer and a hard worker, but at times the family was forced to seek help from the public welfare agencies.

After the death of his parents, Fred became a ward of the county and was placed in a foster home. All his brothers and sisters were separated at this time and Fred has not seen them since.

Fred's foster parents were farmers. He stopped attending grade school when he went to live with them so that he could be of greater help with the chores. These consisted of odd jobs around the farm, since Fred had a nervous disorder and was not allowed to touch the farm machinery. Fred says that his foster parents treated him well but that he always regarded himself as a "hired hand" working for his keep. He led an isolated life, consisting of working, eating and sleeping, but has no complaints, for "after all, I was only living there as a ward of the county." When questioned about his foster mother, he calls her a good housekeeper. His foster father, he recalls, paid little attention to him, but of course, "did not belong to me."

When he was 16 Fred was moved to another foster home. He stayed there only a short time, then left to join the Civilian Conservation Corps. He started drinking at this time. After 9 months he left. At 20 he joined the Army, where he stayed 4 years. He now feels that he should have remained there. His drinking was increasing and he used to get drunk "with the boys" when on leave.

A year after his Army discharge, and while he was employed in a glass works, he was arrested for the first time for public intoxication. Since then he has been arrested twice on that charge.

Fred is now 32. For 6 years he has been working intermittently as a short-order cook at a grill on Skid Row. He complains about the rough customers, the poor food, the continual uproar. He says it is hard on his nerves. He has left his job several times because of "abuse from the customers."

This nervous little man, with a limp and a wild and disheveled appearance, has become a familiar figure on the "street." He lives in the "flop houses," generally where he works, and goes on week-long "benders" with "the boys." He has no contact with women and considers himself a "confirmed bachelor." When he plays—he drinks.

Summary

In this chapter we have investigated the performance of the inebriates in the demanding secondary task roles which relate to education, occupation and marriage. As reflected in their present position in society, performance in secondary roles has not allowed the inebriates to compensate for deficiencies in the primary socialization agencies of the family and the peer group. Traumas which occurred in the family, in the peer group, or in both, have not been alleviated by the establishment of satisfactory primary groups in the marital or occupational fields, or by competent performance in these areas.

Chapter 7

LIFE CAREER PATTERNS

THE CAREER of the chronic police case inebriate is one in which drinking serves the socially handicapped individual as a means for adapting to life conditions which are otherwise harsh, insecure, unrewarding and unproductive of the essentials for human dignity. This type of career is, however, only one of the possible patterns of adjustment, given the combination of conditions in the early life of these men. Repeated incarceration for drunkenness is a terminal phase of a complex process in which the interplay of sociocultural and personality factors have combined to produce this long-run adaptation. For individuals with limited personal resources, the process of progressive adaptive drinking is selective in relation to stress-producing life situations. The process is likewise selective at the community level in that only a certain type of inebriate is handled in this way. The life career pattern of the chronic police case inebriate falls into three definable periods or phases of adjustment: (*a*) the period of preconditioning for dependency, (*b*) the period of dependency formation, and (*c*) the period of confirmed dependency. Each period is marked by a number of characteristic experiences and behavioral manifestations which are a part of the individual's adaptation and may further determine the succeeding adjustment.

PRECONDITIONING FOR DEPENDENCY

The period of preconditioning for dependency is concomitant with undersocialization and serious deprivations in childhood and youth sufficient to limit the individual's chances for successful adult adjustment. During this period the early life career experiences of our men were characterized by one or more of the following traits: (*A*) Nearly half of the families were broken by death, divorce or desertion before the subjects' twentieth birthday. (*B*) Of those who were not from broken homes, four out of five experienced serious loss of family integration. This means rejection by one or both parents or parent substitutes, or an emotional climate in the family so neutral or negative as to be a handicap to personality development. (*C*) The transition from adolescence to adulthood represented a typical adjustment problem for the whole group, with few exceptions. They lacked the usual adolescent experiences, and in most cases were projected at an early age (about 15) into heavy, unskilled work. Seven out of ten left school by the end of the eighth year. The most common observation concerning this period is, "I quit school to go to work." There is an absence of home-centered occupational training; and fathers rarely provided models for adult male occupations. They were projected from semiprotective but poorly integrated family environments into economic functions for which they were ill prepared, from 3 to 5 years earlier than the average American youth.

The evidence concerning this period supports the hypothesis that these men lacked adequate socializing experiences to prepare them to meet society's expectations of the adult. The result was the drift to dependency which is institutionalized in the occupational living patterns of the group.

Conditioning to Alcoholic Dependency

Given the precondition of limited social and psychological development, the period of dependency formation and development of excessive drinking follows. Life situations defining social expectations impinge upon these individuals in such a way that progressive recourse to drinking develops. This period is denoted by one or more patterns of adaptation which will be discussed now.

Occupational maladaptation and mobility is reflected in the incarcerated inebriates' low order of primary occupational skills. Sixty-eight per cent are unskilled, compared to 13 per cent in the general population of the county, and only 3 per cent are skilled in contrast to 22 per cent. Withdrawal from jobs represents a flight pattern of adjustment characteristic of the majority. The life-long pattern of occupational drifting, "quitting the job," periods of unemployment, represent a way of meeting life expectations through the "least common denominator" of effort and competence.

The shift from rural to urban occupations represents one of the major adjustment problems in the life career, since a majority originated in essentially rural communities. Persons from marginal rural social backgrounds, rather than rural per se, constitute an important segment of the group. Migratory work is more characteristic than a direct shift to stable urban occupations.

The lack of continuity in occupational culture is partly a consequence of the social and cultural shift from rural folk environments, which required unskilled labor and were essentially paternalistic in nature, to the competitive-achievement urban situation requiring competence in specific skills. The transition for this group was by way of migratory types of work and a period of extensive geographic mobility.

Extended periods of occupational stability are found in the life careers of some chronic police case inebriates. They are periods in which these men sustained both heavy drinking and hard work in heavy unskilled occupations by virtue of the physical stamina and vigor of youth. This pattern is not inconsistent with the dependency-forming phase of the life career pattern.

The most significant, persistent and universal form of adaptation for these men is the progressive habituation to the excessive use of alcohol to facilitate and mitigate their stress-ridden existence. Theirs is the problem of drifting or "angling" through a complex social system with which they are inadequately prepared to cope. Drinking functions for some as a primary causal influence in the early adult career, and for others as a secondary influence and as a consequence in both the early and adult careers.

Those for whom the function of alcohol was primary showed definable characteristics in the adaptive pattern. The onset of excessive drinking occurred in early adulthood (between 20 and 30 years of age). Their records are marked by early arrests for public intoxication and other offenses involving drinking. In this type of pattern, excessive drinking appears to have been a primary cause of failure or directly adaptive to early failures resulting from other handicaps.

The career in which excessive drinking functions as a secondary cause, or as a consequence of earlier maladjustments, is marked by certain attributes. These men have had relatively stable occupational or marital experiences. The onset of inebriety typically followed crises involving one or more of the following: (a) loss of parent, (b) loss of wife through death, separation or divorce, (c) arrest for crime, (d) loss of job and loss or obsolescence of job skills, and (e) physical decline with age or a physical handicap. These career profiles are further characterized by late arrest records. Alcohol functions in this type of career pattern to adapt the individual to the crises and modes of marginal existence which become more acute with age.

Drinking, whether primary or secondary in function for these careers, occurs in a social and socializing context. It takes place in groups. It is learned with similar associates in establishments which are the major and exclusive places of recreation. They are the "poor man's club" and the only institutions which welcome the transient, the unemployed, the unshaven, not-so-clean, and poorly dressed casual worker. Macrory (34, *p. 625*) says of the "Skid Row Tavern" (as one of five types which he describes) that "It offers little more to the bulk of its patrons than alcoholic beverages and the music of the juke box. The patrons are mostly drifters, homeless single men, transients, vagabonds and alcoholics." Nevertheless these places, with a vested interest in the drinking of these men, provide the only warmth and continual association available to them. This environment is therefore a powerful influence for their learning, maintaining and increasing the use of alcohol. Not only is it easy for the individual to drink, but it is necessary for his integration in the group; he finds it affectively rewarding.

A disproportionate number of the chronic police case inebriates come from native rural and small-town American stock of the lowest socioeconomic group and of Protestant religious backgrounds. They represent a group in this society least socialized in the use of alcohol. They either begin their drinking while at home but under strongly disapproved circumstances, or after leaving home for military service, work camp, Civilian Conservation Corps or the railroad gang, where drinking is least likely to be integrated in familial, religious and communal living.

Institutionalized living of the type noted by Straus and McCarthy (50) is typical of the selective adaptation among the chronic police case inebriates. Tendencies toward dependency inherent in the experiences of childhood, youth and early adulthood are reinforced and supported through adaptation to life in the semiprotective environments of various institutions. These havens are of three types: (*a*) military and semimilitary, such as the Army, Navy, Merchant Marine or Civilian Conservation Corps; (*b*) institutional occupational groups represented in the railroad gang, lumber and fruit camps, lake steamers, and hospitals; and (*c*) shelter institutions such as veterans hospitals, domiciliary homes, and Salvation Army Service Centers.

The minimum requirements for living are met through institutional organizations which relieve the individual of responsibility for coping with problems of food, housing and related needs. Many adjust to institutional living who have never made an independent adult adjustment. They become habituated to dependent living, which further reduces their potential for independent modes of life. It has been noted that the pattern of institutional living is conducive to heavy drinking and tends to confirm dependence on alcohol.

The period of conditioning to alcohol dependency has its repercussions on patterns of adaptation in family living. Nearly six-tenths of the men established independent families by marriage, but these unions were of short duration. Desertion of the family as well as withdrawal from jobs is part of the adaptive flight pattern characteristic of the group. Movement away from and absence of contact with wives, children and kinship members is adaptive to their need for "self"-protection for the failure to meet family expectations. Some of the men, however, remained for extended periods of family support and child rearing. These years of apparent familial and occupation stability were characterized by excessive drinking, and were terminated in nearly all cases by divorce, separation or desertion. The incarcerated inebriate is a nonfamily member of the community and has been for years, whether he ever married or not— and 41 per cent never married compared to 13 per cent in the general male population of the county.

Whatever integrative influence the family ever had has been discontinued. We are dealing with a group of atomized, nonorganized persons for whom the normal (for this group abnormal) stresses of life are handled in semisolitary or institutional living. Their limited opportunities for social participation are within the "poor man's clubs" of Skid Row and the slightly better eat–drink establishments which represent their only opportunity for convivial association in anything resembling a primary group.

For some inebriates this phase in the life career is characterized by crime as a means of adjustment. Criminal activities directly related to the use of alcohol represented a mode of life adjustment in the careers of over one-third of the inmates. Resort to crime appears as an attempt to "make out" in the early phase of the individual's unsuccessful adult career. From this a transition is usually made to excessive drinking as an adaptation to failures, including failure in crime.

Crises related to death of a parent, break-up of marriage, loss of job, obsolescence of occupational skills, financial loss, arrest and incarceration, are accompanied by progressive increase in drinking. Coupled with this is a final condition in the dependency-forming process—the reduced capacity to compete for work opportunities as a result of physical decline related to aging and deterioration related to chronic excessive drinking.

CONFIRMED ALCOHOL DEPENDENCY

The culmination of this type of adaptive pattern is in confirmed dependency on alcohol.[1] This last phase is characterized by several indexes: (a) increased drinking and finally loss of tolerance for alcohol; (b) arrest exclusively for public intoxication, with greater frequency of arrest and shorter intervals between arrests; (c) work of a casual day-labor nature such as dishwashing and "spot" labor jobs; and (d) increased dependency on sheltered living in missions, men's service center facilities, and the like. Confirmed alcohol dependency represents the extreme in the career and is not the necessary culmination for the majority, since half of the men aged over 55 have been arrested for public intoxication fewer than 10 times. The men aged over 55, however, have been arrested for this cause an average of 19 times, indicating the confirmed dependency of half this age group.

CAREER PATTERNS IN PUBLIC INTOXICATION

Using the age at which a man was committed the second time for public intoxication or a drinking-involved offense as a breakpoint, the study group falls into two types which we shall designate the Early Skid and the Late Skid careers.

The Early Skid Career

The Early Skid career pattern involves approximately 50 per cent of the chronic police case inebriates. In this group two-fifths of the men experienced their second incarceration in their twenties and the rest in their early thirties. Only a few had their second imprisonment in the age period 36–39.

---

[1] Whether this dependency is physiological or psychological is still being discussed and debated by physiologists and psychologists (65, 66) and this question, as well as the problem whether we are dealing with "alcohol addiction," fortunately does not need to be settled in the present context.

The Early Skid career pattern is thus one in which the individual establishes his record of public intoxication in his twenties or early thirties. It represents serious maladjustment to early adulthood which extends into middle adulthood. There is an absence of adult occupational adjustment independent of institutional living. The period of alcohol dependency formation is not associated with such stable marital adjustment as may be found in some of the Late Skid career patterns.

The following case history illustrates the Early Skid, public intoxication only, type of career after its full duration.

Case 13. Irwin Murphy is a 50-year-old Irish American born of immigrant and devout Catholic parents in a small New Jersey city. The father, a hard worker and hard drinker, had the responsibility of supporting 11 children. Irwin's parents were "old country" people with whom he never established a close relationship. Raised in the city streets, he quit school at 16 with his parents' approval in order to contribute his share to the family's support.

His drinking began at the age of 20, during Prohibition, with the ingestion of "home brew." At this period he worked as a silversmith (age 18 to 20) and then as a steamfitter (age 20 to 22). Since then, he has worked exclusively as a casual laborer at resorts, railroad camps and Salvation Army shelters, and as a farm laborer and fruit and vegetable picker. Murphy has never been arrested on any charge other than public intoxication. He was first jailed for drunkenness at the age of 27 and since then has been committed 61 times for public intoxication. He served 17 sentences in the first 11 years of his inebriate career, and 45 in the next 11 years. He is thoroughly addicted, drinks anything he can get, and can exercise no control once he starts drinking.

Murphy illustrates the Early Skid career pattern at the late stage of the career. For 22 years he has had nothing but repeated arrests and incarcerations for a pattern that was well established in early adulthood. This history, as typical of the Early Skid career, suggests that here we may be dealing with addiction, whereas the Late Skid career is characterized by excessive nonaddictive drinking conditioned by crises of later life or by physical decline and the relegation of older men to unemployment even in the most marginal types of jobs.

The Early Skid cultural drinker type is illustrated in the following case history.

Case 14. Jim Bales is a 34-year-old Negro who was reared in a cotton-growing community in Tennessee. He remembers his father as a "sport-

ing man" who visited the home occasionally but made no attempt to
support the family. Jim and his six brothers, some of whom were half-
brothers by another father, lived with an aunt and the whole family
worked as share croppers in cotton. He remembers his aunt as a good
woman with whom he was happy, with plenty of food to eat. His father
never figured in his boyhood development, although the mother did
the best she could until her death when Jim was 7. He left school to
go to work at 11 years of age but can barely read the headlines in the
newspaper and just manages to sign his name.

Jim's drinking started in the Army at the age of 24. He served 5 years
in the Army and was once court-martialed for drinking-related misbe-
havior. After leaving the Army with an honorable discharge, he found
that his wife had squandered the pay he had sent home and he decided
to leave her. Jim has one child. No divorce was secured; he just wandered
off. He now lives in a common-law relationship with a girl who often
works with him at farm labor. They do not contemplate marriage. He
prefers to drink with women or in mixed groups. His drinking usually
ends in a fight. During his last drinking episode he threw a bottle through
the window of a bar on Front Street. He finds the police stricter in
Rochester than in New York City, which makes him more vulnerable
to arrest.

When working, Jim does not usually want to drink. He has never had
trouble getting work, but has lost several jobs as a result of drinking.

Jim lived in a southern farm community until inducted into military
service, and thinks his troubles started with his entrance into the Army.
His criminal record began in Memphis in 1947, at the age of 27, when
he was jailed for drunkenness and disorderly behavior. He had three
commitments in the next 2 years, all for drunkenness and related offenses.
The record shows 15 commitments for public intoxication or related
offenses since his first incarceration in 1947. He reasons that he is not
an alcoholic because he eats when he drinks and is able to stop when he
wants to. In this respect, Jim is not like some of the men who say they
come to jail to stop drinking.

The history of this 34-year-old Negro represents a subtype of
the Early Skid pattern, which we shall refer to as the cultural
drinker pattern. Bales is a nonaddictive excessive drinker, a "spree"
or "Saturday night" drinker, who is vulnerable to arrest because of
his race and his manifestation of the tendency of the lower-class
Negro to indulge in aggressive disorderly behavior when drinking.
In his career we see the following sequence: (a) dependency
developed under a matriarchial family situation; (b) shift to institutional living in military service; (c) parallel development of
drinking and institutional living; (d) marital crisis; (e) shift from
a protective paternalistic environment which tolerated and sup-

ported an established pattern of drinking and aggressive behavior to the urban North where the police arrest him on drinking occasions when he becomes a visible public nuisance. There is little evidence of addiction and he typifies the nonaddictive periodic excessive drinker characteristic of his subcultural grouping.

The Early Skid, maladjusted personality type may manifest any of the following: (a) only public intoxication in his record; (b) primarily criminal involvements not related to drinking; (c) mixed nondrinking criminal offenses and public intoxication; (d) a shift from primarily a nondrinking criminal career to one primarily of public intoxication. The following case history illustrates the type of maladjusted personality with a serious drinking problem as well as serious crime early in the record, shifting to an exclusively public-intoxication pattern.

Case 15. Andrew O'Hara, a 47-year-old white man, explains the circumstances of his past life in the following manner: He had a happy uneventful childhood and graduated from a high school in New Jersey. His parents were devout Catholics, and they sent him to Notre Dame in the hope that he would enter the priesthood. Andrew had the idea, however, of becoming a doctor. After 2 years at Notre Dame he quit and renounced his faith. His work record after college was at first excellent; he became superintendent of the small plant at which he was employed. Heavy drinking began at this period, with lowering of personal and social standards, reaching its culmination in conviction on a charge of forgery. This was a major crisis-evoking situation in his life. He spent 5 years in a state prison, during which time his wife divorced him. Repeated alcoholic bouts interspersed with attempts at "mission preaching" make up his life now. Excessive drinking, he feels, is the cause of all his troubles, since from the beginning his consumption was excessive and drunkenness usually followed.

Recently, O'Hara has been passing himself off as an ex-Catholic, now converted to Protestantism, who peddles his "testimony" to certain types of missions. These missions invite him to preach and provide room and board. During these sequences he abstains, but subsequent tensions with other staff members, as he explains it, cause him to "hit the skids" again. He exhibits considerable understanding of the mind and emotions of the "mission stiffs" to whom he gives the altar call. His last exploit occurred with the Heart Hope Mission, recently established in Rochester, in the organization of which he played an active part. The duties assigned to him consisted of preaching and giving the altar call, but the inevitable happened. Tensions with other staff members built up as they began to complain about his smoking and attempted to exorcise the devil out of him. O'Hara felt that his resignation was in order. This was followed by a drinking bout, leading to his present incarceration.

His criminal career began in 1937, at the age of 30, when he was arrested for petty larceny. Since then he has been convicted 31 times. Between 1937 and 1946 (ages 30 to 39) the convictions involved both petty and serious crimes: petit larceny (2 counts); forgery (2 counts); public intoxication (3 counts); disorderly conduct (2 counts); burglary (2 counts). From 1947 to the present he has had 19 convictions, all for public intoxication.

O'Hara's history illustrates the Early Skid type of career in which the determining factor is in the maladjusted personality so gross as to appear to be the primary cause of the early decline. Three major characteristics of the Early Skid type are evident in this case: (a) the predominance of the personality component; (b) involvement in serious crime in early adulthood concomitant with excessive drinking; and (c) a functional shift in adaptation from excessive drinking and serious crime to public intoxication. This is a typical latter adaptation of the criminally involved Early Skid pattern of adjustment.

Another Early Skid pattern relates to the criminal arrest sequence. In this type, the early phases of the career are characterized by arrests not only for felonies but for public intoxication as well; in late adulthood the pattern, as in the preceding type, shifts to arrests for public intoxication only. This career pattern is marked by serious maladaptation in early adulthood including the following characteristics: (a) rapid acceleration of the alcohol dependency formation period; (b) absence of even minimal occupational adjustment in early adulthood, but rather an effort to obtain a livelihood by criminal pursuits; (c) early excessive pathological drinking; (d) a mixture of arrests for public intoxication and serious crime; and (e) confirmed alcohol dependency before the age of 36 with a beginning of the pattern of arrest on charges of public intoxication only. The following case history illustrates this pattern.

Case 16. Joe Smith is a 40-year-old white man who was reared chiefly by his grandmother. His father, working in a construction crew, was absent from home at least 7 months out of the year, and his mother accompanied her husband on these trips, leaving the child to the care of his grandmother. She was good to him, even indulgent. Joe always liked school and was active in sports; he liked to pitch and for a time played baseball as a semiprofessional but was not good enough to make a career of it. He was somewhat handicapped by a weak muscle in the left eye which necessitated wearing glasses and gave him the appearance of being cross-eyed.

After completing high school, Joe went to work. His father wanted him to learn to operate a power shovel and to find work in the construction business, but he did not like it. He learned the trade of wool finisher and worked at this until 24 years of age, when it was decided that he should go to college. It was his mother's wish and the family finances at that time made it possible. He attended college until drafted into the Army. At first he did not like the Army, but gradually he adjusted. He "lost his stripes," however, more than once; he would get along for a period and then "blow his top" and get drunk.

Joe's father died when he was 25 and his mother died just before he was discharged from the service. Since he had no home to go to, Smith headed for the West Coast. He worked up and down the West Coast at odd jobs, then came to Omaha, Nebraska. There he took up with an old Army friend and together they began to "run hot cars." They were apprehended in this business of stolen automobiles and committed to a Federal prison.

Throughout this Smith had been drinking heavily and he wondered whether or not he might be an alcoholic. After leaving the Federal penitentiary, he found it almost impossible to hold a job because of his prison record. He relates several experiences in which his work was satisfactory but he was dismissed because of his record. He concluded then that he could work only at "spot jobs." Smith detests restaurant work and would like something better, but because of his prison record and his continual drinking, no one, he thinks, will give him a chance.

He now considers himself an alcoholic but has been unable to find any substitute for drink. Alcoholics Anonymous has not helped, since he does not feel at home with the group. Smith thinks that many of them are not "real alcoholics" but "just a bunch of bums going along for the ride." He does not like that. He believes that drinking is associated with morals and that if an alcoholic truly changes his life he should change it all the way.

Smith has been arrested 23 times and has served 3 prison terms for auto theft. Since the age of 24 he has been arrested 15 times for public intoxication. His last 10 arrests, since 1944 when he was 33, have all been for public intoxication.

The Late Skid Career

The Late Skid career pattern is defined by the postponement of the minimum record of two incarcerations for public intoxication until the forties and even fifties. This career type encompasses 50 per cent of the men in the group if the age of 37 (for experiencing the second arrest) is used as the dividing point. The median age of this group at the second arrest was 44. The confirming period for the Late Skid men was after age 40, the heaviest concentration (30 per cent) occurring between 40 and 45, the least between 36

and 39 (only 5 per cent), and 11 per cent past the age of 50. The
Early Skid and Late Skid career types represent a bimodal frequency distribution with the critical ages concentrated in the early
thirties (Early Skid 30 to 35) and early forties (Late Skid 40 to 45).
The great range in the ages of serious involvement, 40 years between
the earliest at 20 and the latest at 61, points to the heterogeneity
of the group in this respect.

The period of alcohol dependency development is often marked
in this pattern by extended periods of occupational and family stability. Since this period is accompanied by drinking, it must nevertheless be regarded as part of the conditioning period for alcohol
dependency. The Late Skid career is marked by the prolongation
of this phase.

More apparent in the Late Skid career is the physical decline
of the man who is having great difficulty in maintaining his economic needs through marginal types of employment. Younger men
replace him on the casual day-labor jobs. His drinking increases and
finally his tolerance for alcohol declines.[2] He appears to fit more
nearly the nonaddictive excessive drinking pattern than the addictive.

The following case history illustrates this career type:

Case 17. Edward Francis is a 56-year-old native white American of
Scotch-Irish parentage. His father was a successful farmer who worked
his sons hard on the farm. His mother died when he was 12. He had no
close friends in grade school and quit high school at 15 because "father
needed me on the farm." At 17 he married the only girl he had ever
courted. She was a teacher, 10 years older than he. He rented a farm,
later bought it, and operated it successfully for 7 years until he sold out
and went into the automobile business because his wife was dissatisfied
with farm life. He preferred the farm, but wanted to please her.

Francis started drinking 2 years after he entered the automobile
business, at the age of 26. He operated the automobile agency for 11
years, during which time four children were born to the couple. During
the depression, at the age of 37, he lost everything. He separated from
his wife a year later, and in the next year started drinking heavily,
after 13 years of moderate drinking. His first arrest for public intoxication
came at the age of 46, some 7 years after his separation from his wife
and family. He blames his wife for his downfall—"a nagger under hard-
ship."

During this latter period Francis became a casual worker, primarily in

---

[2] On the occurrence of loss of tolerance to alcohol late in the career of inebriety,
see Jellinek (26).

institutional settings. He worked as a painter, then for 6 years as a hospital attendant. Subsequently he has worked 5 years on the railroad and 3 years in Salvation Army shelters. He likes institutional work and thinks he is too old for hard labor. Since his first arrest at the age of 46, he has had 16 arrests for public intoxication over a period of 10 years. He is now 56 and has had no contact with his family during these 10 years.

Among the Late Skid group are some men with a very late public intoxication record and only a few offenses. This type of career indicates the concomitant symptoms of physical decline, loss of tolerance to alcohol, and greater psychological dependence on alcohol with increased age. The following case history illustrates this pattern.

Case 18. Peter McCarthy, an affable 53-year-old Irish-American born in New York City, has a record of only two incarcerations—both for public intoxication in the last year. There is no evidence of serious emotional deprivation in his early family life. His father was a steady worker and good provider, not given to excessive drinking. When his mother first came to this country from Ireland she worked as a maid, but after her marriage she never worked outside the home. Peter's family resided in a deteriorated tenement district in New York where "you had to be tough to survive."

At the age of 14, due to economic pressures, Peter quit school to go to work. Most of his career has been spent in construction work at casual labor. However, he has done some railroad work and farm labor, and for 5 years was a hospital attendant. The last job he held before his incarceration was in a bowling alley, setting pins.

McCarthy has never married, never considered marriage, although when he was 25 he went out with a girl for 2 years. He began drinking during the Prohibition era at the age of 27 but excessive intake started only recently. His drinking is consistent with lengthy residence about Skid Row and the type of work he does, casual labor. He is a nonaddictive excessive drinker.

The history of this man demonstrates a career of the Late-Late Skid type, involving no criminal offenses other than public intoxication, and only two of these at the age of 53. These factors characterize this type: (*a*) absence of criminal involvement; (*b*) relatively adequate occupational career; (*c*) nonaddictive excessive drinking as an adaptation to physical and occupational decline; (*d*) drinking as a secondary cause of decline. The pattern is merely one of the life adaptations of the single, aging, unemployable male who is effectively isolated from an organized family or institutional living which would afford him protection in his declining years.

The Late Skid crime-to-public-intoxication career pattern is one in which arrests for serious crimes distinguish early adulthood and arrests in late adulthood are for public intoxication only. The criminal career is frequently prior to the onset of drinking and without arrest for public intoxication. The early adult career is also marked by absence of any stable occupational adjustment, and the shift from criminal arrest to arrest for public intoxication is complete. The following case illustrates this career pattern.

Case 19. Pat Brady was born in Detroit into a large family of six children. His mother was born in Ireland. His father died when he was 10. The mother went to work for 3 years, then married. Pat did not get along with his step-father, although the other children did not have the same difficulty. He was the leader of a gang of boys who were delinquents. Pat completed grade school and then ran away. He was arrested at 14 for automobile theft and sentenced to the reformatory for 4 years. When he was 17 his mother died, and during the same year he was returned to the reformatory for automobile theft. Between 1927 and 1936 (age 17 to 26) he served sentences for automobile theft, attempted burglary (two counts) and forgery. His first incarceration for public intoxication occurred in 1944, at the age of 37 and after an interlude of 8 years without any arrests.

Brady did not begin to drink until he was 24. He has had six arrests for public intoxication between 1944 and 1953. He had little trouble with his drinking until after he underwent surgery of the stomach a few years ago. Now he finds it impossible to "hold his liquor" as he once did. As he grows older and as it becomes more difficult for him to make a living, his drinking has increased. As an ex-convict he has no trade and has engaged only in casual labor. He now washes dishes and hates it. Eventually he gets "disgusted with life" and goes on a binge.

Chapter 8

WHAT CAN BE DONE

UNTIL THIS POINT we have attempted to be nonevaluative in viewing the behavior and life career of the chronic police case inebriate. We have eschewed a moralistic indictment of their activities as well as a social-reform plea on their behalf. We have tried to describe them and to understand why they behave as they do. We have sought to picture the broad development of their life career from their family of origin to their present confinement in a county penitentiary on conviction for public intoxication. Admittedly, we have neither understood nor explained all their behavior, for this is an impossibility in the present state of knowledge. We feel, however, that this study allows certain conclusions to be drawn concerning the present system of handling the chronic police case inebriates and concerning changes that should be instituted in this system.

THE PRESENT POLICY

Given present-day social and cultural definitions and philosophy as they are represented in the law, the individual who is convicted of public intoxication or a related offense must be punished for his deviant behavior, although many judges use every means at their disposal to avoid imprisonment until treatment methods available in the community have been exhausted. Community attitudes, however, define the public inebriate as a nuisance who must be either fined or jailed. Some segments of the community seem to feel that punishment by incarceration or a stiff monetary penalty will induce the individual to change his style of living and way of life; that in the penitentiary he will grow penitent of his "sins" and become a sober member of the community on his release.

The results of our investigation negate completely the assumption that incarceration acts as a deterrent to the chronic public inebriate. Let us see just how successful jailing has been in preventing these men from resorting to drunkenness. Of the 1,357 men committed to the Monroe County Penitentiary in 1954 on charges of public intoxication or allied offenses, only 5 were newcomers to prison life. About one-third of these men—455 to be

exact—were there for their second to tenth round. Nearly 6 out
of 10 (801 men) had been committed from 10 to 25 times to a
penal institution, and 96 men had served 25 or more jail terms. Our
study group, a random sample of their kind, includes men who have
been arrested 81, 90 and 110 times for public intoxication. There
is no question about it: jailing has not deterred them from further
public drunkenness.

In brief, these men are not rehabilitated in the penal institution.
Any belief that punishing them by a jail term in the county penitentiary will help solve their problem is an illusion. It must be
recognized that repeated jailing, as a socially and legally accepted
philosophy in the community for reforming the chronic inebriate,
has been and will continue to be a failure—aptly termed the revolving door policy—unless radical changes are instituted by the society.

In the jails of the nation the present emphasis is upon custodial
care rather than rehabilitation of the public inebriate. Our investigation indicates that many of these men could be rehabilitated
if treatment were available to them as part of an integrated program. In the present penitentiary system some men do not even
receive systematic medical examinations to determine their physical
condition and what essential physical treatments and corrections
are required. There is no legitimate excuse for the incarceration
of the tubercular alcoholic; his place is in the sanitarium. Some
steps are now being taken to correct this in Rochester and elsewhere.
Those who are mentally ill belong in the state hospitals. The paucity
of psychiatric service makes any effective mental health care un-
available to this group. Rarely is there an assessment by a competent
individual, such as a social worker, which might help determine
what assets an individual has for rehabilitation and allow the development of a classification scheme for handling various types of
offenders.

Release procedure that would aid in the inebriate's subsequent
community adjustment is nonexistent. This is in sharp contrast
with the practice in releasing prisoners convicted of felonies in New
York State. A system of parole planning reduces the risks of unemployment or homelessness. But the more numerous short-term misdemeanants, upon release, are provided with little more than fare
to the county seat or to the city from which they were sentenced.
There is almost complete absence of systematic parole planning
which would include the location of employment and a residence

and provision of essentials for living at least until the first pay is earned. Is it any surprise, therefore, that the inebriate is often arrested for public intoxication within 24 to 48 hours after his release? Thus the vicious circle is retrodden, culminating in the institutionalized offender—one who develops a social and psychological dependency on the institution and begins to view it as his home.

The present indictment of the system of incarcerating the chronic police case inebriates is of course not a criticism of the officials of the penitentiary where this study was conducted. The personnel of this institution are doing the best job possible, given present public attitudes concerning the public inebriate. They are only performing the functions society has created, and this applies to the staffs of many like institutions throughout the land. Our observations are directed against the philosophy of handling the chronic inebriate, not the personnel assigned this duty.

Our treatment of the chronic inebriate reflects long-established customs, moral sentiments and legal rules of our society. They are rooted in a centuries-old philosophy which regarded drunkenness primarily as a moral problem. This belief has resulted in handling the inebriate according to practices which are at least a century behind those employed in other fields of social welfare. The newer concept of alcoholism as a social, mental and physical illness is in gross conflict with punishment and confinement for the habitual public inebriate.

RECOMMENDATIONS

1. *New Approach.* Given the failure of the present system to cope with the problem of the chronic police case inebriate, a new system or philosophy should be envisioned built on the concept of treatment and rehabilitation instead of punishment and custodial care. The present system hardly does more than allow the inmate to build up his physical resources for a new drinking bout upon his release and then to lapse back into the hands of the police.

2. *A Treatment Center* should be created for the reception of the chronic public inebriate. This means that they should be removed from the jails and penal institutions as the mentally ill in this country were removed from the jails during the last century. Given the present state of knowledge concerning alcoholism, the

time is ripe now for such a change. The present system is not only inefficient in terms of the excessive cost of jailing an offender 30, 40 or 50 times, but is a direct negation of this society's humanitarian philosophy toward people who are beset by social, mental and physical problems.

3. *Systematic Treatment* has not been tried as a method of dealing with the problems of excessive drinking of over 90 per cent of these men. The following are essential factors in the operation of any treatment–rehabilitation center:

A. *Medical and physical rehabilitation:* Some prisoners are sick with tuberculosis, venereal disease, hemorrhoids or other physical maladies. This investigation has shown that after necessary minor and major physical corrections at least 80 per cent of these men are employable at some task.

B. *Psychological rehabilitation:* Both psychiatric and psychological evaluations are essential to determine the internal resources of the individual for meeting external reality. Psychotics should be sent to their proper place in mental hospitals. For the majority, therapeutic devices can be instituted, such as group therapy and individual counseling.

C. *Social rehabilitation:* The present system does little for the social rehabilitation of the inebriate during the period of incarceration. The treatment center with an accent on rehabilitation can be the group context within which the individual gains insight and develops new solutions to his problems. A social worker can record a case history of the inebriate in which assets for rehabilitation are evaluated and an individual plan for rehabilitation is prescribed. For those who are interested, Alcoholics Anonymous groups should be encouraged, and occupational therapy should be provided for those who can benefit.

4. *Release Procedure.* Release from the treatment center should be based on a system of parole planning in which each individual participates in a plan of recovery.

A. *Social work:* In the treatment of mental illness, convalescent care or parole planning has become an important part of release procedure. In the treatment center for inebriates a social worker can provide the focus around which a systematic plan is worked out for the release of each man to society. The plan should include provision of a job, housing and financial aid until first wages are received, and contact with community resources such as Alcoholics Anonymous, clinic facilities and other social agencies.

B. *Halfway house:* For those whose histories show a confirmed pattern of dependence upon institutional living, release to independent living may only be a gradual process. For the excessively dependent person the "halfway" house advanced as a therapeutic device by students in this field would be a useful part of the program. A sudden complete severance from the treatment center would be traumatic for some. The "halfway" house cushions the shock of the movement from slavish dependency by providing supportive independence in the form of a residence in the city to which they can return after work, where they can take their meals, and participate in some forms of recreation and social living. The pattern of dependency is so deeply ingrained in some men after 30 or 40 years that they may never advance beyond this stage; but they may at least be made economically self-supporting.

5. *Differentiation of Types.* There are several different types of men among the chronic police case inebriates who will require different kinds of treatment. This can be discerned from adequate social histories which are part of the intake procedure of a treatment center. These social histories will allow the development of a system of classification which will be useful to all personnel engaged in the work of rehabilitation.

A. *The Negro:* Negroes are migrating to various urban centers in growing numbers. Our study shows that, given present conditions, greatly increased numbers of Negroes will fill the city jails on conviction for public intoxication. These numbers can be reduced substantially if each community will develop a policy of aiding the less advantaged Negro migrants. Most communities are without such a policy, and Negroes in general are relegated to the slums and blighted areas of the city. They also have the least favorable opportunities for employment. They need constructive programs now, rather than platitudes about brotherhood.

There should be specific education programs for all public officials and private agencies on the special problems of the southern
rural Negroes who migrate to the North or West. As all previous
studies in this field have shown, the Negro is the victim of discriminatory treatment in arrest and commitment. Eighteen per
cent of the men in our sample were Negro, compared to 2 per
cent Negroes in the county population—a reflection partly of the
higher vulnerability of the Negro to police and court action.

B. *The older offender* with few arrests for public intoxication
and no other history of criminal involvement (one of the "Late
Skid" types): The major problem here is physical decline which
affects occupational abilities; the drinking problem may be secondary. Special consideration must be given to the dependency
needs of these individuals. Certain institutions, such as the
County Home, are now available for this type, but the way of
life of these men is so incompatible with this sort of institution
that they cannot adjust to it. The special problem of relating
this type of individual to an institution should be reexamined.
Our study shows that these men are highly amenable to institutional living but not suited to many of the existent institutions.
The Men's Service Center in Rochester, New York, has had considerable success in removing many of the negative features of
institutional living for this type of man. This group also needs
special attention for physical maladies due to aging.

C. *The mentally disturbed:* For men, especially in the younger
age brackets, with psychological disturbances as manifested in
their social and criminal histories, deep-going psychotherapy is
indicated. Their histories show, however, that the disturbances
were frequently noticeable in the childhood or adolescent phases
of their personality development. Mental hygiene in early life
is still the best means of coping with behavior disorders.

6. *Research.* A program of continuous research in the problem
area of alcoholism, within which the chronic police case inebriate
is only one part, is essential. We hope that state and community
agencies will be able to utilize this study in formulating basic
policies for rehabilitation of these inebriates. We suggest here only
a few of the many research topics which have been engendered
in the course of this investigation.

A. Systematic evaluation of the results of the different measures now being tried for the rehabilitation of the chronic police case inebriate and the general category of alcoholics should be expanded.

B. Research should not be confined to a study of individuals who have developed the pattern of excessive drinking or alcoholism. Our interests should reach beyond merely salvaging and repairing individuals who have serious problems, although this is a necessary activity. Research is indicated to obtain an understanding of the deep-seated origins of the behavior disorder, particularly in two areas:

(a) *Adolescence:* One hypothesis that might be tested is that the socially isolated adolescents of lower-class Irish background and lower-class background of certain Protestant groups have a greater chance of becoming chronic police case inebriates than do adolescents who are not members of these groups and who are incorporated into clique groups.

(b) *Institutional living:* The role of institutional living contexts in initiating and supporting excessive drinking warrants investigation.

7. *Conclusion.* We recommend that the program of treatment take into account the realities of status and life circumstance which brought the chronic police case inebriate to his present condition. Our study has shown him to be the product of a limited social environment and a man who never attained more than a minimum of integration in society. He is and has always been at the bottom of the social and economic ladder: he is isolated, uprooted, unattached, disorganized, demoralized and homeless, and it is in this context that he drinks to excess. As such, admittedly through his own behavior, he is the least respected member of the community and his treatment by the community has at best been negative and expedient. He never attained, or has lost, the necessary respect and sense of human dignity on which any successful program of treatment and rehabilitation must be based. He is captive in a sequence of lack or loss of self-esteem, producing behavior which causes him to be further disesteemed. Unless this cycle is partially reversed, we doubt that any positive results can be attained.

A program of treatment must strike at his dependency needs and recognize his needs for human approval and self-respect. The program must therefore be administered by persons who are professionally competent to minister to his needs, who can create an environment of human warmth, and who are personally interested in the inebriate as a human worthy of respect. Within such a context the goals for rehabilitation must be realistic. We may eventually find that the rehabilitation of only a majority of this group is a notable achievement. Even so, if the remaining minority are simply maintained according to standards consistent with morality and decency in our time, it will do credit to the community which first makes such a contribution.

Bibliography

1. Alcoholics Anonymous. The Story of How Many Thousands of Men and Women Have Recovered from Alcoholism. 2d ed. New York; Alcoholics Anonymous Publishing; 1955.
2. ANDERSON, N. The Hobo: The Sociology of the Homeless Man. Chicago; University of Chicago Press; 1923.
3. BACON, S. D. Inebriety, Social Integration and Marriage. (Memoirs of the Section on Alcohol Studies, Yale University, No. 2.) New Haven; Hillhouse Press; 1949. Also in: Quart. J. Stud. Alc. 5: 86–125, 303–339, 1944.
4. BACON, S. D. Alcoholism, 1941–1951. A survey of activities in research, education and therapy. IV. Social science research. Quart. J. Stud. Alc. 13: 453–460, 1952.
5. BALES, R. F. The "Fixation Factor" in Alcohol Addiction: An Hypothesis Derived from a Comparative Study of Irish and Jewish Social Norms. Doctoral dissertation; Harvard University; 1944.
6. BALES, R. F. Cultural differences in rates of alcoholism. Quart. J. Stud. Alc. 6: 480–499, 1946.
7. BANAY, R. S. Alcoholism and crime. Quart. J. Stud. Alc. 2: 686–716, 1942.
8. BUCHANAN, M. Experience in an Outpatient Clinic with Prolonged Treatment of Court Referrals. Concord; Division on Alcoholism, New Hampshire State Department of Health; 1954.
9. BURGESS, E. W. and LOCKE, H. J. The Family. New York; American Book Co.; 1945.
10. COOLEY, C. H. Social Organization. New York; Scribner's; 1909.
11. COOLEY, C. H. Human Nature and the Social Order. New York; Scribner's; 1922.
12. DAVIS, A. Comments on Mr. Erikson's Paper. In: Human Development Bulletin, Fifth Annual Symposium. Chicago; Committee on Human Development; 1954.
13. DAVIS, A. and DOLLARD, J. Children of Bondage. Washington; American Council on Education; 1940.
14. DAVIS, A., GARDNER, B. and GARDNER, M. R. Deep South. Chicago; University of Chicago Press; 1941.
15. DAVIS, K. Human Society. New York; Macmillan; 1949.
16. ERIKSON, E. Childhood and Society. New York; Norton; 1950.
17. FEENEY, F. E., MINDLIN, D. F., MINEAR, V. H. and SHORT, E. E. The challenge of the Skid Row alcoholic. A social, psychological and psychiatric comparison of chronically jailed alcoholics and cooperative alcoholic clinic patients. Quart. J. Stud. Alc. 16: 645–667, 1955.
18. FLOCH, M. Imprisoned abnormal drinkers. Application of the Bowman–Jellinek classification schedule to an institutional sample. Quart. J. Stud. Alc. 7: 518–566, 1947.

19. GLAD, D. D. Attitudes and experiences of American-Jewish and American-Irish youths as related to differences in adult rates of inebriety. Quart. J. Stud. Alc. **8:** 406–472, 1947.
20. GLUECK, S. and GLUECK, E. One Thousand Juvenile Delinquents. Cambridge; Harvard University Press; 1934.
21. GORDON, C. W. The Social System of the High School. Glencoe, Ill.; Free Press; 1957.
22. HALL, J. Drunkenness as a criminal offense. Quart. J. Stud. Alc. **1:** 751–766, 1941.
23. HAVIGHURST, R. J. Developmental Tasks and Education. New York; Longmans-Green; 1953.
24. HOLLINGSHEAD, A. B. Elmtown's Youth. New York; Wiley; 1949.
25. JACKSON, J. and CONNOR, R. The Skid Road alcoholic. Quart. J. Stud. Alc. **14:** 468–486, 1953.
26. JELLINEK, E. M. Phases of alcohol addiction. Quart. J. Stud. Alc. **13:** 673–684, 1952.
27. JELLINEK, E. M., ISBELL, H., LUNDQUIST, G., TIEBOUT, H. M., DUCHÊNE, H., MARDONES, J. and MACLEOD, L. D. The "craving" for alcohol. A symposium by members of the WHO Expert Committees on Mental Health and on Alcohol. Quart. J. Stud. Alc. **16:** 34–66, 1955.
28. KELLER, M. and EFRON, V. The prevalence of alcoholism. Quart. J. Stud. Alc. **16:** 619–644, 1955.
29. KEPHART, W. M. Drinking and marital disruption. A research note. Quart. J. Stud. Alc. **15:** 63–73, 1954.
30. KISER, C. V. and WHELPTON, P. K. Social and psychological factors affecting families. Milbank Mem. Fd quart. Bull. **22:** 72–105, 1944.
31. LANDMAN, R. Studies of drinking in Jewish culture. *III.* Drinking patterns of children and adolescents attending religious schools. Quart. J. Stud. Alc. **13:** 87–94, 1952.
32. LEVINE, J. The sexual adjustment of alcoholics. A clinical study of a selected sample. Quart. J. Stud. Alc. **16:** 675–680, 1955.
33. LOLLI, G., SERIANNI, E., GOLDER, G. M. and LUZZATTO-FEGIZ, P. Alcohol in Italian Culture. Food and Wine in Relation to Sobriety among Italians and Italian Americans. (Monographs of the Yale Center of Alcohol Studies, No. 3.) New Haven; Publications Division, Yale Center of Alcohol Studies; and Glencoe, Ill; Free Press; 1958.
34. MACRORY, B. E. The tavern and the community. Quart. J. Stud. Alc. **13:** 609–637, 1952.
35. MILLER, N. E. and DOLLARD, J. Social Learning and Imitation. New Haven; Yale University Press; 1941.
36. MURPHY, M. M. Social class differences in intellectual characteristics of alcoholics. Quart. J. Stud. Alc. **14:** 192–196, 1953.
37. MURTAGH, J. M. The New York City program for the Skid Row alcoholic. In: Publication of the Institute on the Skid Row Alcoholic. New York; National Committee on Alcoholism; 1956.

38. MYERSON, A. Alcohol: A study of social ambivalence. Quart. J. Stud. Alc. **1**: 13–20, 1940.
39. PARREIRAS, D., LOLLI, G. and GOLDER, G. M. Choice of alcoholic beverage among 500 alcoholics in Brazil. Quart. J. Stud. Alc. **17**: 629–632, 1956.
40. PITTMAN, D. J. The Chronic Police Case Inebriate. Doctoral dissertation; University of Chicago; 1956.
41. RECKLESS, W. R. The Crime Problem. New York; Appleton-Century-Crofts; 1950.
42. RILEY, J. W. and MARDEN, C. F. The social pattern of alcoholic drinking. Quart. J. Stud. Alc. **8**: 265–273, 1947.
43. SCHILDER, P. The psychogenesis of alcoholism. Quart. J. Stud. Alc. **2**: 277–292, 1941.
44. SMITH, T. The alcoholic offender and the community. Master's thesis; Syracuse University; 1954.
45. SNYDER, C. R. Alcohol and the Jews. A Cultural Study of Drinking and Sobriety. (Monographs of the Yale Center of Alcohol Studies, No. 1.) New Haven; Publications Division, Yale Center of Alcohol Studies; and Glencoe, Ill.; Free Press; 1958.
46. STRAUS, R. Alcohol and the homeless man. Quart. J. Stud. Alc. **7**: 360–404, 1946.
47. STRAUS, R. Social Stability and Disruption in Alcoholism. Boston; Division of Health Information, Massachusetts Department of Public Health; 1952.
48. STRAUS, R. Alcoholism. In: ROSE, A. M., ed. Mental Health and Mental Disorder; ch. 29. New York; Norton; 1955.
49. STRAUS, R. and BACON, S. D. Alcoholism and social stability. A study of occupational integration in 2,023 male clinic patients. Quart. J. Stud. Alc. **12**: 231–260, 1951.
50. STRAUS, R. and McCARTHY, R. G. Nonaddictive pathological drinking patterns of homeless men. Quart. J. Stud. Alc. **12**: 601–611, 1951.
51. SULLIVAN, H. S. The Interpersonal Theory of Psychiatry. New York; Norton; 1953.
52. SUTHERLAND, E. H. and CRESSEY, D. R. Principles of Criminology. Chicago; Lippincott; 1955.
53. SUTHERLAND, E. and LOCKE, H. J. Twenty Thousand Homeless Men. Chicago; Lippincott; 1936.
54. SUTHERLAND, E., SCHROEDER, H. G. and TORDELLA, C. L. Personality traits and the alcoholic. A critique of existing studies. Quart. J. Stud. Alc. **11**: 547–561, 1950.
55. SYME, L. Personality characteristics and the alcoholic. A critique of current studies. Quart. J. Stud. Alc. **18**: 288–302, 1957.
56. TAFT, D. Criminology. New York; Macmillan; 1950.
57. TAPPAN, P. Who is the criminal? Amer. sociol. Rev. **12**: 96–102, 1947.
58. TERRY, J., LOLLI, G. and GOLDER, G. M. Choice of alcoholic beverage among 531 alcoholics in California. Quart. J. Stud. Alc. **18**: 417–428, 1957.

59. TRICE, H. M. A study of the process of affiliation with Alcoholics Anonymous. Quart. J. Stud. Alc. **18:** 39–54, 1957.
60. ULLMAN, A. D. The first drinking experience of addictive and of "normal" drinkers. Quart. J. Stud. Alc. **14:** 181–191, 1953.
61. [UTAH STATE BOARD ON ALCOHOLISM.] A study of arrests for drunkenness in Salt Lake City. (Current Notes.) Quart. J. Stud. Alc. **11:** 695–701, 1950.
62. VOGEL, S. An interpretation of medical and psychiatric approaches in the treatment of alcoholism. Quart. J. Stud. Alc. **14:** 620–631, 1953.
63. WARNER, W. L., MEEKER, M. and EELLS, K. Social Class in America. Chicago; Science Research Associates; 1949.
64. WHYTE, W. F. Street Corner Society. Chicago; University of Chicago Press; 1943.
65. WORLD HEALTH ORGANIZATION, EXPERT COMMITTEE ON MENTAL HEALTH. Report on the First Session of the Alcoholism Subcommittee. World Hlth Org. Tech. Rep. Ser., No. 42, 1951.
66. WORLD HEALTH ORGANIZATION, EXPERT COMMITTEE ON MENTAL HEALTH. Alcoholism Subcommittee, Second Report. World Hlth Org. Tech. Rep. Ser., No. 48, 1952.

Index

Date Due